I Walked Away

An Expatriate's Guide to Living Cheaply in Thailand

by Michael Ziesing

Introduction by Mike Gunderloy

Loompanics Unlimited
Port Townsend, Washington

I Walked Away: An Expatriate's Guide to Living Cheaply in Thailand

© 1996 by Michael Ziesing

Published by:
Loompanics Unlimited
PO Box 1197
Port Townsend, WA 98368
Loompanics Unlimited is a division of Loompanics Enterprises, Inc.

Cover artwork by Terry LaBan

ISBN 1-55950-139-1
Library of Congress Card Catalog 95-82083

Contents

Acknowledgments

No adventure is undertaken alone. Everyone needs help in life. I would like to thank the following people for helping me.

In America:
Without Dave the mailman, student and friend, everything would have been impossible. Deborah, one of the greatest writers on the planet, who always came through when I really needed it. Friends like Reijo helped me stay in tough. Childhood buddies like Ken, Annie and Patty listened and stuck with me.

I needed help in Thailand too:
Det has provided more than help. She has done more for me than any woman in my life, save my mother.

There is my Thai family.

Eddie, my son, keeps me young.

I am indebted to my in-laws for exploding every single stereotype created by cynical ex-pats.

And then there is my family.

My mother has been a rock. A source of support that was constant and essential. Even though we are further apart than ever, we are closer. My father has pushed the limits of his understanding and love. I am proud that he's lived up to the things he taught me — marching to the beat and defending the right. My brother marches to his own particular drummer. He has never stopped encouraging and helping. I'm proud that he's a hippie at heart and that his radio is soapless. Zack and Isaiah are my boys. I hope for their understanding in the face of a society that celebrates victimization. Cindy had written when others haven't. She's my Gemini twin sister. Abe is my buddy, harmonicas to hoops. Kate is a fine girl who will kiss the sky. Paul has never, ever, been a bummer.

Some of the friends and family I am so indebted to may not agree with, or approve of, or like what I have done with my life. Of that, I'm not sure. But they are tolerant. For that, most of all, I thank them.

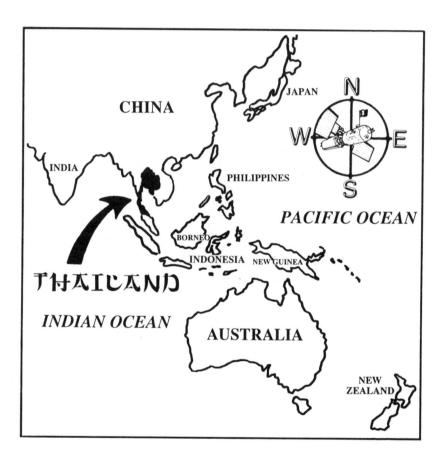

About the Author

Michael Ziesing was born in El Paso, Texas in 1946. His father was an army officer, so he lived all over the U.S., as well as in Germany and Italy, when he was a boy. He never lost his wanderlust.

He has been a chef's assistant in a Chinese restaurant, farm worker, construction worker, psychiatric aide, Navy hospital corps-

Michael Ziesing in Thailand

man, sailor, flea market entrepreneur, bookseller, publisher, philosophy professor, publican and ESL (English as a Second Language) teacher.

He graduated from Moorhead State University (Minnesota) in 1971 with a B.A. in Philosophy, and did his graduate work at the University of Connecticut, graduating with an M.A. in Philosophy in 1972.

He is the author of *The Scarlet Q,* and co-editor (with Mike Gunderloy) of *Anarchy and the End of History.* He was the editor of the long-running anarchist periodical *Instead of a Magazine.*

Besides reading, writing and teaching, he likes to drink beer, eat peanuts and watch boxing, American football or UConn basketball.

Shortly after completing this book, he accepted a position on the Humanities Faculty for a university in Bangkok. He divides his time between Bangkok and his home in rural Northeast Thailand.

"There exist only about a half dozen beer-mystic, anarcho-Taoists in the world and Michael Ziesing is one of them."
Hakim Bey

Introduction
by Mike Gunderloy

I don't know precisely where in Thailand Mike Ziesing lives. Nor do I know whether he has a couch in his little house there, although I rather doubt it.

However, I do know two things with the utmost certainty. The first is that the door's not locked. The second is that if Mike were ever to come home from a trip to get his visa renewed and find me sleeping on his (probably non-existent) couch, he'd greet me warmly, offer me a beer and not be all that surprised by my presence.

You see, Mike is one of those truly good friends that the lucky person will pick up in the course of a life. We got to know each other rather well when we were both gadding about what passed for a U.S. anarchist movement in the late eighties. We edited a book together, we drank beer together, we slept in the same hotel room from time to time. The drive from Boston down to Willimantic (where he then lived) was always a wonderful one for me, because I knew at the other end there was a kindred spirit and a cold beer. That's an excellent combination. The good vegetarian food was an added bonus.

Of course, times change, and most of us change with them. Mike and I both drifted away from the "movement" (which, in retrospect, doesn't seem to have been moving so much as running in place) and have gotten on with our lives. Am I surprised that he's in rural Thailand, the possessions of his previous life spread around the community? No more than he will be to learn that I'm in rural Virginia, writing computer software for a living and surrounded by more stuff than ever before in my life. We've each continued on our own paths to peace and prosperity, and although I no doubt find it much easier to buy a variety of beer than Mike does, I think on the whole he got the better of the deal.

Sure, there are those who will use the usual loaded terms to describe the lives of these two aging anarchists. "Drop out" and "sell out" come immediately to mind. I could make the usual academic arguments about retreat being a means of advance, or about worldly success serving to show others that you're doing something worth emulating. But I won't. There eventually comes a time when you realize that changing yourself into a better person is more rewarding and more effective than trying to change others. Mike in his little house and I in my larger one aren't out there oppressing people. If everyone else could honestly say the same, the world would be a better place.

Oh, and Mike – if you're ever in Virginia, you're still welcome to crash on my couch, buddy.

Mike Gunderloy
"Claymont"
Summer 1995

𝒫reface

Many people dream of chucking it all, walking away and starting a new life in an exotic country. This is the story of how I did that and what I've learned. It is a true story, but it is frank and, to some extent, subjective. It is a story of the joys and pitfalls of living life in a tropical, easygoing, lovely country that is populated with beautiful people. It's the story of life as an expatriate in Thailand.

Some who dream of starting over in Thailand might envision moving to a tropical island, for example Ko Samui or Phuket — two popular vacation destinations in the South of the country. It could be that others imagine a home in Chiang Mai in the North, a farm in Northeast Thailand, or even crowded, polluted, but always intriguing Bangkok. Thailand has something to offer everyone, even those who don't know the country.

In 1992, I left it all. From the United States, I moved to the island of Phuket in Southern Thailand. When I lived in Phuket, vacationers frequently told me they were jealous that I was able to do something they wished they could do. They often asked me a lot of questions about how I had been able to do it. Some of the questions were practical, some theoretical and some personal.

The purpose of this book is to share my experiences with those who dream about doing what I have done. In that regard, it is personal and intuitive. I make no claims about being an expert on Thai business law, customs, language or even culture. What I do have is an enthusiasm and respect for Thailand as well as a love of learning. I will share with you what I have learned, and some of the things I have done and seen during my adventure in Thailand.

For many people, including me, Thailand is an extraordinary place populated by delightful people who are always ready to have fun, to smile and who refuse to be seduced into the tight schedules and deadlines so common in the West. For most of the year, the weather is gorgeous — if you enjoy a balmy, tropical climate. By and large, Thailand is an economical place to live. If you have been to Thailand, you have been fortunate enough to experience all this firsthand. If you have not been to Thailand, and you have grown tired of the hustle and bustle of the Western world, you should, by all means, give serious thought to visiting this enchanting country.

The aim of this book, however, is not to sing the praises of Thailand. Many other books do that quite well. Rather, what I hope to accomplish is to give you some insight into what it is like to live, and perhaps work, here. I hope to get you to think about what you are doing or yearning to do even if that involves saying things that you disagree with. In that regard I have tried to pull no punches when it comes to the difficulties, as well as the joys, of starting a new life in Southeast Asia. You may not agree with some of the things that I say. That is fine. Certainly you must ultimately decide matters for yourself. It is, after all, your own personal journey. But I hope that you agree that if you want to live in Thailand, a new understanding and a new way of thinking are important.

This book is written from the perspective of a divorced, middle-aged (and then some) man. If you have been to Thailand, you have some idea of what that might mean. I have not glossed over anything that accompanies the experiences of such a man. Political correctness might be OK for those who can afford the luxury of theorizing rather than *doing*. However, as a Westerner relocating to Thailand, the reality of everyday life is more important than the speculative agenda known as "political correctness." Consequently, I have opted for frankness in this book, rather than sugar-coated and comfortable political platitudes.

Further, political correctness is a relative notion. What is politically correct in the West, might not be in the East. Those with a Western political agenda have no more right to tell Thais what or how to do things than other Westerners with an equally superior attitude. Thailand is their country and a fabulous one it is. Do-gooders claim to want to help Thai people improve themselves. Cynical redneck types think the Thai way of doing things is ignorant. Both of these sorts of people are wrong — no matter how well-meaning (or racist) their motives may be. I prefer to leave things to the Thai people and learn from them. You will find that to be the underlying theme of this book.

Thais tend to be somewhat fatalistic and accepting in their approach to life. Consequently, they have not bought into the "recovery movement" so popular in the West. They are much less likely to feel that they have been "victimized," and are more willing to take responsibility for their actions and the consequences. They are not whiners and complainers. Psychotherapy is not big in Thailand, and I suspect that is because most people neither need nor want it. Thais recognize that everything is "up to you," and this is a frequently heard phrase. In my view, one of the great lessons Westerners can learn from Thai people is the lesson of individual responsibility.

While I agree with those who hold that everything we say and do in life is, in some sense, political, I do not intend for this book to be a tract on how we or anyone else *should* see the world. It is not a book about changing Thailand or the foreigners who visit or live here. It is a book about what *is*, not a book about what *ought* to be. But, having said that, I need to add that it is a book about the way we — *guests* in Thailand — *ought* to behave. In my humble opinion, we must, in nearly all things, accept Thailand the way it is and adjust *our* behavior and attitudes.

I remember getting a letter from my brother Mark. He said that I was living my dream. I wrote back to him and said that it was not so much a dream as an adventure. Adventures have dragons of assorted varieties. Sometimes they're unpleasant dragons of a type found in the West — bureaucracy, for example. There are personal problems, sickness and many others things that are no fun. Thailand is not heaven, and Thais don't claim that it is. In this book, I will write a lot about the different dragons you will find. I will tell you how to avoid running into them, if possible, and some of the things that you can do should you encounter one. In that regard, there are many things in this book that may seem negative or critical. And, of course, Thailand has problems like any country does. But I hope that I have avoided painting a negative or cynical picture of this marvelous country. I do not enjoy being around ex-pats who endlessly complain and criticize a country they freely chose to live in. I elected to live here and I am free to leave anytime. I enjoy living here and do not have any desire to move away. I do, indeed, have a wonderful life. Those ex-pats who are fond of being negative about Thailand need to take a look at their passport and see where they are from.

Sometimes it seems as though 90% of the letters to the *Bangkok Post* involve complaining about something in Thailand or telling Thais how they ought to do things. The things in Thailand that need changing, and there are some, the Thai people are perfectly capable of doing themselves. Many of the problems that Thailand has — deforestation, destruction of coral reefs, and even litter — are the direct result of Western values being imposed or adopted. More of the same doesn't strike me as particularly wise.

At the same time, as someone who is perhaps dreaming about relocating to Thailand, you need to be made aware of some of the difficulties that you will run into. Living in a place is not at all the same as vacationing in a place. Some of the things that you liked as a visitor may annoy you as a resident. In addition, as a country with a government, police force, food, customs, culture and language that you are completely unaccustomed to, knowledge and then patience are essential for you to live here successfully and happily. Patience you will have to acquire on your own. Maybe I can help you learn a little something. I hope so.

Chapter One
Getting Started

Some things in life we think about for a long time, and others come as quickly as a tropical rain storm. Some things, unbeknownst to us, have been happening for a long time. It's just that we become *aware of them in a flash.*

It was the summer of 1992, and I went to teach my summer *Philosophies of the Orient* class at Eastern Connecticut State University on Thursday, as I had every night that week. I had returned the previous Saturday from a trip to Thailand, and was still suffering a bit from jet lag. I suspect that part of my heart and soul were still on the other side of the earth as well. I had traveled to Thailand again and again over the past few years.

As I walked to my car at about 8:30 PM that evening, it was still light outside. It occurred to me that it was about 7:30 "tomorrow" morning in Thailand. I felt very much at peace, happy to be teaching and — pardon the expression — very mellow. When I was about halfway to my car — maybe 50 yards from it — I had a realization. What I realized was a commitment to make a change in my life. It was going to be a rather drastic change, but it was one that I knew I was going to make. When I got home, I sat down and started a new journal. Here is the first entry:

Willimantic, Connecticut, June 11, 1992
    Tonight I decided to get rid of everything I own except what I can fit into a backpack. I expect that to take six months to a year. I

am also leaving my teaching jobs — my primary source of income. After all that is taken care of, I am moving to Thailand. I have no specific plans relative to earning a living and there is nothing lined up. I am not well connected.

This decision is not a reaction to anything or anyone. I am a happy person, love teaching, like Willimantic — where I have been for about 20 years — and New England. I have many friends in the area, including the person dearest to my heart. My children, who do not live with me, are also in the area although they are essentially "grown" (17 and 19 years old).[1] I am not running away. There is no person in Thailand to whom I am going.

When I made that journal entry there were, of course, some things that I knew which you do not. At the time, I was not a young man. In fact, I was five days away from my 46th birthday. Even by flexible standards, that is middle-aged. There was essentially no way that I could not at least partially burn some of my bridges. A leave of absence, sabbatical or anything of that sort was not possible for me. I was a part-time, full-time college teacher. That is, I taught part-time at several places. As long as I stayed in the area, I was assured of earning a decent living by teaching. If I left, there was no telling what would happen. I did not have anything vaguely resembling job security. Of course, the positive flip-side of security is freedom. That was something I did have. But I guess all of us do on some level. We are free — aren't we?

I gradually began telling my friends about my decision. I didn't get the "mid-life crisis" reaction quite as often as I thought I would. In fact, the most common reaction, from men and women alike, was: "I'm jealous." The next most common reaction was: "My God! Thailand! Political problems! AIDS! The world economy!"[2] But mostly what I got was a lot of support.

---

1 Prior to moving to Thailand, my children, along with their mother, moved over a thousand miles away to Wisconsin.

2 People who don't know the country, often react that way — largely as a result of misinformation acquired from the U.S. media. While AIDS is a problem, as it is nearly everywhere, politically and economically Thailand is quite stable.

I began the process of starting over.

Among the first things that I began doing was figuring how to get rid of stuff. I began to think of it as "shedding matter." It turned out to be deeply interesting, and a tremendous learning experience. I'd like to say that my motive for shedding matter was purely philosophical, spiritual and psychological, but the truth is that some of it was financial. I had some bills to pay and, being reasonably mature, realized that I would need money to survive after I left Connecticut. What could I sell? What *should* I sell, and how would I go about doing it?

It is pretty amazing — you know, the stuff we accumulate over the years. Even though I think few Americans would see me as a materialistic person, it struck me that I had a lot to unload. Once, when I was away in Asia for a couple of months, I had asked my neighbors to watch my house for me and feed my cat. They had never been in the house before I left. I was talking to them one day when I got back and one of them said, "You live a pretty basic life, don't you?" I assumed that had something to do with the stuff I had (or maybe didn't have). I figured it was pretty adequate: A modest but sound six-room Cape house, a 1986 Chevy Spectrum that ran just fine, a 1984 Honda Shadow motorcycle, a lot of books, records, a TV, stereo, refrigerator and a few other things. I had taken a number of pictures over the years and picked up a few other interesting things that decorated my walls. I am not a clotheshorse, so there wasn't much in that department. But it was there. Stuff! Dead weight. What to do?

The first thing to go was the motorcycle. It wasn't hard to sell, either practically or emotionally. It was warm, and the season to sell it. I figured I'd better do it while the doing was good. After going without it for an entire summer, I had no regrets, but did miss it somewhat on sunny days, when the thought of the wind moving across my face as I leaned into a curve was very appealing.

The next thing to begin going were my records. I thought that would be difficult, but it wasn't. I have a friend who has a funky shop in downtown Willimantic who agreed to sell my records on consignment. I was skeptical, and while she denied it, I think she was, too. But to my surprise, the records began to sell, and then took off like wildfire. We were both happy. I was helping her and she was helping me. One day she said to me, "Michael, selling your records is making my summer financially. But when you left the other day, I felt really weird. 'This is Michael Ziesing's life that I'm selling!' I said to myself."

I reassured her that it was OK, but as I drove away, I thought about what she'd said. I didn't have to think too long before I realized that there was no way she was selling my life. True, the record collection contained music that had been purchased over a span of more than 30 years. I still had the very first album I'd ever bought — a Roy Orbison record. I'd purchased Bob Dylan's first album when it was his *only* album. Some of the recorded music I had moved from Paradise, California, to Philadelphia, to Key West, to Moorhead, Minnesota, to Connecticut. But it was not my life. Stuff can't, and consequently shouldn't, be one's life. I know who bought many of the records that sold, and feel real good about the direction they went.

The next thing I began to work on was books. Eventually, I found an excellent used bookshop in Marlborough, Connecticut. Run by a cranky old book-lover who puffs on a cigar and drinks shots of whiskey as he "goes into a deep trance" determining how much to offer for the books, it was a real find. This man was fair, and my books would find new good homes.

Of course, there were many other little things which were given away to friends or the Salvation Army. Although a lot were small and/or worthless, some of them brought sad smiles to my face as I said good-bye to them: There were my kids' toys from when they were little, my Navy uniforms, an Army jacket my dad wore in Korea and gave to my oldest son on a trip we made together to the Southwest desert, a special gray jersey I wore during a very romantic time in my life. And, of course, there was much more. A day didn't go by when I didn't say, "My God, what about that?" It wasn't that I didn't want to let go. I did. But sometimes I felt like the archer in a Zen or Taoist tale. I'd take aim at the target, trying to make sure that my aim was true. But creating the tension and then letting go is what makes the arrow fly. I really wanted that arrow to fly and was more than willing to let go. I just hoped my aim was true.

Some things couldn't be let go of because I would need them in the time before my final departure. Basic furniture, clothes, reference books and so forth, would have to wait until the last minute. One thing that was startling was to have empirical evidence of the garbage that one accumulates. I made one or two trips a week to the dump for several weeks, throwing stuff away that no one would want.

Within days after my decision, I determined that I would use the two weeks that I had between the end of summer session and the beginning of the fall semester to take another trip to Thailand. This time it would be with a different mental perspective. I wanted to get more specifics about actually living in Thailand — nuts and bolts about costs, jobs and so forth. Fortunately, I had accumulated enough frequent flyer mileage to make the trip for free. So, off I went, making my fourth trip to the land of smiles in the space of two years.

Even though, in economic terms, the flight was free, there is a major price to be paid in terms of time. From Hartford, it takes almost exactly twenty-four hours to get to Bangkok. Leaving at about 10 AM you arrive at about 10 PM — the next day! Taking into account the eleven hour time difference (when the U.S. is on Daylight Savings Time), it is a marathon flight. Eventually, you kind of lose track of time and go off into mental cruise control. Detroit, Tokyo and then Bangkok. Overpopulated, polluted, traffic-jammed Bangkok. It nearly felt like I was home.

I spent about five days in the city, and I learned this: Accommodations can be as little a $100 per month for a room with a bed and a bathroom. These were not acceptable basic accommodations, though. Even to me, a budget traveler who is used to three-dollar-a-night guest houses and has no problem with Oriental-style toilets, they were slum-like. They were filthy, way on the outskirts of Bangkok, and just not what I was looking for.

Next I checked out the possibility of a long-term hotel arrangement. A small room in a decent hotel goes for about $300 per month. That isn't bad when you consider that it includes air conditioning, phone, television, utilities, very good security and an excellent location. Another option is a one room, furnished apartment. There are plenty of these, and they can be had for as little as $180 to $250 a month. You must pay your own electric bill, but phone service is usually included.

Next was the issue of making a living.

English teaching jobs in Bangkok seemed to be plentiful. There were numerous ads in the *Bangkok Post*. Yes, I did suspect that had something to do with the fact that it was August, but it was still promising. I checked some of them out. Pay ranged from $6 an hour to a bit over $1,000 per month. The former were more tutoring-type jobs and semi-fly-by-night operations. The latter were at schools and hotels, and included a very handy piece of paper — a work permit. There were jobs in between. At that point, my feeling was that given my degrees and teaching experience, I would have no trouble getting a job. How good that job would be was another matter, but I felt that I was employable.

The next thing on my agenda was to check out the possibility of starting a business in Thailand. I had several ideas, but the two at the top of my list were opening a bookstore or a bar. I had been a bookseller with my brother in Willimantic for many years. I know the book business, and still love it. In Bangkok, and in a few outlying places (Chiang Mai in the North, for example), there are English-language bookshops and publishers. The bar idea came to me because, particularly at some of the beaches in Thailand, there are open-air, thatched-roofed "beer bars." Some of them are right smack on the beach. Tourism in Thailand is a fairly big business and, in many areas, it is still growing. The notion of sitting back in a tropical paradise watching the world go by seemed like a pretty good way of spending my "middle ages." So I went to Phuket, a resort island that is big enough to handle a fair amount of tourism and still not be spoiled.

When I arrived in Phuket, I was pleasantly surprised to run into a friend I had met on a previous trip. Steve is a retired Australian jockey who has tried to make a living in Malaysia in the waterproofing business. He had temporarily put that endeavor on hold and had decided to buy a bar at Patong Beach, there in Phuket. He was more than willing to talk and share information with me. For several days, often over a Singha or Kloster beer, we talked and looked things over. Here is what I learned: Only Thais can own real property in Thailand. Buying a bar, or any business, involves leasing the property.

Depending on the property and the length of the lease, that can run anywhere from $5,000 to $40,000 (and up). $5,000 will get you a lease for a year or more. Monthly rent of about one to four hundred bucks must be paid in addition to that. Still, all in all, it isn't bad.

Living in Phuket is also much cheaper than in Bangkok. I didn't look into hotels or apartments. Again, I got all the basic information I needed from Steve. He rented a house with several bedrooms for just a bit over $200 a month. That put things in perspective. He offered to keep his ears open for a reasonable rental while I wrapped things up back in Connecticut.

Phuket also offered another possibility for keeping body and soul together. Some of the fancy hotels in the area hired English teachers. Granted, sometimes was just for the "high season" — when a new crop of workers comes in — but it was a prospect. Salaries for these kind of jobs are $600 to $1,000 a month, plus room and board.

Because I love the real Thailand and felt it wouldn't be a good idea to leave without somewhat checking out that option, I also took a trip to Trang — a very untouristed town in Southern Thailand. I wanted to get the feel of what it would be like to start from scratch in a business — say, a guest-house kind of thing — in a place where there was essentially no ex-pat or tourist activity of any kind. A guest house in a location like this would be aimed more at independent budget travelers than at tourists — people who wanted to get off the beaten track. In the end, I came to the conclusion that starting a business in a location like that would be possible but very difficult without a close and trustworthy Thai friend. The main reasons for this are the language barrier and absolute unfamiliarity with Thai business practices and laws. The big plus side of a place like this is the fact that it is incredibly cheap to live, as is true of all of the real Thailand. What do I mean by incredibly cheap? A person could live a quiet and basic life for $100 a month. It would mean giving up a lot of amenities, but it is certainly possible.

In the end, I decided to start my new life in Phuket. I'd go there for a month or two and listen. True, Phuket was a tourist center, but that is misleading. There are still unspoiled and sparsely populated beaches on the island. There are Thai villages and temples where life is essentially unchanged. The real Thailand is still nearby and, in fact, all around you, if you just pay attention. For a place to live, at least at first, there was something to be said for having other ex-pats around and having access to phones, faxes, copiers, etc. In addition, I could check the *Bangkok Post* out regularly for teaching jobs in Bangkok and elsewhere, and pursue them if it seemed like a good idea. Finally, there is another big plus to Southern Thailand — it is quick and cheap to go to Malaysia for passport/visa business. From the North, a place I also like a lot, it would be more time-consuming and expensive.

My two weeks in Thailand went by quickly, but I felt they were worthwhile. Back home, I busied myself with a full load of classes to keep my mind occupied. While it was true that my heart and head were, in some sense, in Thailand, I still enjoyed my final semester of teaching. I didn't dread it or count the hours. It was a wonderful distraction and a privilege to do. It was a part of me, and I worried how I would handle it if I started a life that didn't involve teaching. But, for that last semester, I felt good that I was there in Connecticut with my students as I looked forward to and planned the changes in my life. Still, when I was not thinking and planning and preparing for my classes, I felt "homesick" for Thailand. I know it sounds strange, but it is true. I am not exaggerating even a little.

In the final weeks before my departure, I rented my house to a solid friend and former student. He also bought a lot of the remaining furniture. Then, on the eve of the winter solstice of 1992, I left Connecticut. It would be a year without a winter. I left the jacket I wore to the airport on the plane after it landed in Bangkok. I wouldn't be needing it.

That first year would come and go, and I would miss another winter. It was nearly two years before I returned to the country of my birth, and as of this writing I still have not returned to Connecticut.

I lived on the island of Phuket in Southern Thailand for almost two years. I had a bar for a year, but that was a nightmare. I love my beer too much to make it a job, and I wasn't cut out to be a publican — especially in Thailand. I write more about owning a bar later in the book.

There are other ways to make a living in Phuket. I taught English at a small language school for about a year. It wasn't university-level philosophy, but it was rewarding and educational, and put a few beloved beers in the refrigerator. And yes, I did have a refrigerator as well as a stove. After living without hot water for over a year, I bought a small heater for the shower. My Thai-style home in Phuket cost me $220 a month, utilities included. There were three bedrooms. Nothing else was a room. The kitchen and living room were open-air. I occasionally rented out the extra bedroom to a traveler. I had no car, no telephone, no satellite dish, no air conditioning, no health insurance. Neither did I have taxes or insurance bills or traffic jams.

I went to one of Phuket's scores of beaches at least once a week, and to the market twice a week. I went out drinking two or three nights a week. I wrote and read, and sat on my porch every evening and watched the sunset through the coconut and banana trees as the water buffalo roamed in the field beyond.

I met a fine woman and moved to rural Northeast Thailand in October of 1994. The physical setting is different, but the lifestyle is similar. No late nights or bars here, however. That's fine by me.

As an adventure, life in Thailand has not been without difficulties and assorted bugaboos. Many of them are most unpleasant. Neither is my life without personal problems and occasional dealings with bureaucrats, functionaries, and even once in a while authority figures. Nothing serious, mind you. Just life. Things get broken and are sometimes difficult to get fixed. Sometimes I get sick. Financially, there is always a concern, as there would be anywhere on earth for a guy like me. But then, nobody said that moving to the other side of the world would be a picnic.

When, at the end of the day, I'm sitting and watching the sunset or listening to the rain pour onto the tin roof of my house, I love Thailand and Thai people. I have no plans to return to America. I have no plans not to, either.

I think I have learned to be a more spontaneous and accepting person. Perhaps that is age. I think it is Thailand.

One thing is certain, though. I've never regretted the realization I had in that parking lot 12 time zones and 10,000 miles away.

Chapter Two
Running Away?

Have you wondered *why* you want to start a new life in Thailand? Before you go, it will be one of the questions most frequently asked of you. What's your answer?

The ancient Greek philosopher Plato said that there were three kinds of people — those who are motivated by money, those who are motivated by fame and those who are motivated by knowledge. Fame is related to love. Those who want fame want to be loved — by as many people as possible. Plato went on to say that it is what we want ultimately that defines our character. If, for example, you want knowledge in order to acquire money, what you really want is money. The question is, what do we want *for its own sake?* Which of these things moves you to Thailand?

Probably one of the most common notions about expatriates is that they are people who are running away from something — that they have problems. No doubt, there is a rather large grain of truth in that belief, but it is certainly not universally the case. Still, the issue needs to be addressed.

I remember meeting an ex-pat in Phuket. He didn't live in Thailand, but rather the United Arabs Emirates where he was a programmer for English-language lessons. A frequent visitor to Thailand, he was about 50, and had failed both in business and marriage in his native England. He contended that all expatriates — without exception — were running away. We had some pretty heavy-duty philosophical debates about it, but never resolved the issue.

Running away from something, or even leaving a place because you hate it, is probably not the best motive for moving to Thailand. It isn't the best motive for moving anywhere, for that matter. But I'm not going to write about that side of things — at least not directly. What I do want to write about is people who have come here for negative reasons. It is important to know about them because you will meet a plethora of such people, and they may have a impact on your life.

A huge percentage of the ex-pats who live in Phuket, Pattaya and Bangkok are troubled, and to some extent, desperate people. The first problem they have is drinking too much. (Please remember that I am a person who drinks my share of beers every day, so I am not a prude about such things.) Raging inebriates who drink all night and all day and habitually get violent are not the sort of friends who will help you. The problem is, of course, that it isn't always easy to recognize such people. That might be because you have remained on "holiday mode" or at least "Saturday-night mode." You reckon these guys are out having a good time, just as you are. They aren't. They're drunks. Drunks lie, cheat and steal. But these guys have been around Thailand for a spell. They might actually seem amiable. They could start off helping you — introduce you around, help you find a place to live and even get an actual job. In fact, it is *likely* that they will help you. But remember, when they look at you, they don't see an ex-pat, a friend, a drinking buddy. They see someone with money who is very naïve about living in Thailand. Soon, they will be talking about a business venture they are in. They need a partner. Or, they will be more crass and ask to borrow money — maybe a lot of money. You probably aren't used to this. You'd better get used to it in a hurry if you want to live in Thailand. And, if you are a person like me who hates to say "no," you'd better correct that quickly, too. Learning how to say "no" is perhaps the most important lesson you'll learn in Thailand.

People who have spent any time at all in Thailand are used to hearing stories about how ex-pats and frequent visitors get ripped off by Thais — especially Thai women. I'll write more about that later. For now, my message is this: Be careful with expatriates — especially heavy-drinking types, people who seem a little too anxious to help you, and bar owners. There are some good bar owners. One of my best friends on earth is both a heavy drinker *and* a bar owner. I'd do anything for him — including loan him money. But, in my personal experience, I have had far more problems with ex-pats (many of them bar owners) than I have had with Thai people. Be nice, but be careful. Make friends slowly, and trust people even more slowly.

Another negative personality type is the cynical ex-pat who believes that he has been done wrong by a Thai — again, most often a Thai lady. I find it difficult to sympathize with a 45-year-old man who married an illiterate 19-year-old Thai "bar girl" and got taken to the cleaners. But you will meet many such people. Instead of learning from their mistakes, what they have done is adopt a universally negative attitude about Thailand. There are hundreds of variations of this self-inflicted disease: Woman-hating, stereotyping, accusations of greed or lack of conscience and trustworthiness are just a few of them. The best inoculation against these mind viruses is a be careful, but not paranoid, attitude. Most particularly, be careful with the cynical ex-pats. They'll do you a lot more damage than any Thai. Quite plainly, the cynical Thai-bashing ex-pat ought to go home. They are not only bad for Thailand, but they do grave damage to those ex-pats who live in Thailand because they love it.

Here are two brief stories about bad experiences friends of mine had with ex-pats. The names and locations have been changed. The essence and morals of the stories are based on actual fact.

Bob was from New Zealand, and in his early fifties. He'd had a stationery business in the country of his birth, and had spent every vacation he'd had over the past three years in Thailand. He decided that his modest nest egg was sufficient to allow him to move to Thailand permanently. He had no specific plans, but had thought about opening a bar. He ended up doing this in Pattaya. Before opening the bar, he met an Englishman named Graham. While it seemed to him that Graham drank a lot, it didn't appear to be a problem. When Bob decided to buy a small bar, Graham said he knew a woman who would make an excellent cashier. She had been a cashier before and knew all the ropes — licensing, taxes, etc. The woman, whose name was Noi, happened to be Graham's girlfriend.

The author (left) enjoys Thai night life with a bar girl and a friend from Down Under.

Bob paid $6,000 for the bar, and spent another $4,000 fixing it up. Graham, who had worked for free beer the week before the opening, began to present bills for his work. In some cases the bills were for things that friends would have done for free — copying music tapes, for example. But Bob didn't think much about it. Also, partly to head off trouble, he had told Graham that he could drink for cost. He never saw Graham paying for his whiskey, but Noi assured him that he did. Bob believed her, and forgot about it for a while.

Graham swilled Black Label whiskey daily, 20 to 30 drinks a day. Sometimes more. When he was drunk he got aggressive and tried to pick fights — a couple of times, even with Bob. Several times he got into fights in the bar — with Thais and farangs alike. One time a Thai woman beat him to a bloody pulp.

On a couple of occasions, Graham invited Bob to his home for dinner. When Bob finished eating, Graham presented him with a bill for the food.

Even though Bob's bar was moderately successful, he didn't make any money. It seemed that whenever he had a really good day, Noi would inform him that there was a tax bill or a charge for some service that Graham had rendered. The funny thing was, on several occasions Noi was forced to take some time off. In one case, it was for a couple of weeks. When Noi wasn't there and the young backup cashier was in charge, Bob made good money.

To make a long story short, Graham and Noi were ripping Bob off big-time. It took a year for Bob to figure this out because he was such a trusting soul. Graham had drunk thousands of dollars worth of free Black Label, and Noi had put thousands of dollars in her pocket. The straw that broke the camel's back was a motorbike. Bob had loaned his motorbike to Graham on several occasions. He never asked him for money that wasn't offered. Then Graham had a motorbike accident that totaled the bike, but, with a drunk's luck, did no damage to himself. When Graham didn't offer to pay for the repairs, Bob came right out and asked for the money. "Don't have it, matey," was the reply.

Bob sold the bar. He'd lost a fair amount of money, but learned a valuable lesson.

Barry was from Australia. He'd spent a lot of time in Thailand on holiday as well. Much of that time, in addition to the money he spent, was in a bar in Bangkok owned by a Canadian named Joe. Barry had gotten to know Joe pretty well. He liked him and trusted him. One day Joe approached Barry and asked if he wanted to be partners in his bar. He was sure, given some improvements, that they could increase the profit and that they would both benefit. Barry agreed, and on the basis of a handshake, put up $20,000. Joe assured Barry that within six months he would begin getting a return on his investment. Joe expanded the bar, and bought a pool table, satellite dish and big TV. Business began to boom. The place was packed-out every night. Six months later, Barry, who was on an extended holiday, returned. He was extremely happy when he saw the bar and the obviously great business it was doing. After hanging around for a couple of weeks, Barry asked Joe if there was any money for him. Joe said no, there was nothing. Barry believed Joe, and even though the bar was filled with customers nightly for the remaining month of Barry's holiday, he never got a cent. Two more times this happened. Finally, after several more visits and Joe's continued insistence that the bar was not making any money, Barry confronted him. Joe refused to give Barry a penny, and told him that if he didn't like it to go to court. Since Barry had not so much as one word in writing, that would have been futile. He was $20,000 poorer, but hopefully wiser for his experience.

Finally, just a personal note about owning a bar. Ask yourself if that is what you really want to do. It is an extremely difficult proposition, and very hard work. There are very few happy bar owners. If you think that owning a bar is simply a matter of chatting with friends, or drinking and flirting with women as you did when you came to Thailand on holiday, please think again. Owning a bar is hard on your body and even harder on your soul. Unless you are in partnership with someone you can absolutely trust, the odds are overwhelming that you will be cheated. Unless you are there nearly all the time, supervising virtually every move, it is certain that you will be ripped off. Many people who work for you will probably be troubled and uneducated, and they will drink a lot. They are under enormous pressure to make money. The people who come to your bar will often be lonely, troubled, heavy drinkers who are either on holiday and know little about Thailand or are the cynical ex-pat types. That is not a job or a business so much as it is a powder keg. Throw in corruption of assorted varieties, greedy landlords and miscellaneous other monsters, and you have an incident waiting to happen. My advice about opening or buying a bar is this: Don't!

There are happy stories.

The older Scotsman who was lucky enough to find a solid woman. She stuck with him, even though he lost his money as well as his health. She worked in their modest bar and he slowly recovered. They made enough money back to buy a small house up-country.

There was the middle-aged Welshman who was ripped off by his lady but was smart enough to blame himself. He gradually got his finances back together, and somehow managed to hold onto his bar. Happy as a clam, because he was a natural-born publican, he now has a decent new girlfriend, an active business and a fine bungalow.

In the end, as all Thais know, what you do is "up to you."

Chapter Three
Where In Thailand?

Place! What *place* should it be?

Having a sense of place might be one of the most important things in life. Having a sense of place is knowing where we are. Where we truly are.

The first decision that you will have to make when you move is where you want to live in Thailand. This chapter is written for those who are largely starting from scratch — those who have no friends, connections, sweetheart or anything else to direct them to a particular spot. It will help if you have some familiarity with Thailand and have traveled it a bit, but that is not essential.

Most probably, you will consider moving to one of the following places: Bangkok, Pattaya, Phuket, Chiang Mai or Ko Samui. The reason for this is that you have been there and enjoyed yourself. You might even know a few people there. That is a plus — provided they're the right kind of people.

I know something about Phuket because I lived there for nearly two years. I know something about Bangkok because I have spent a lot of time there and have friends who live there. I have been to Pattaya, Chiang Mai and Ko Samui, but only as a traveler. Depending on what you are looking for and how open-minded you are, all of these places are wonderful to visit. On the other hand, having a holiday in a place and living there are two different kettles of fish entirely. Of course, you know that in your head. The trick is to incorporate it into your heart. The holiday lifestyle of many single men who come to Thailand is probably not the best way to lead one's life on a full-time basis. Some people have the money, physical constitution and desire to do that. Many don't. Believe it or not, most people can get sick and tired (literally) of getting drunk every night, shagging women, going to bed at 5 in the morning and sleeping until 1 PM. It gets old, and it gets old fast — for most of us anyway. Keep that in mind if you are thinking about a place like Pattaya.

I remember seeing wire-service newspaper reports in the U.S. written by A.P. or U.P.I. correspondents based in Pattaya. Man, I was jealous. Imagine that, I thought, living in Pattaya, and getting paid for it. I'm not jealous any longer. It is very difficult, if not impossible, to avoid the holiday lifestyle, even if you want to.

If Pattaya, or Patong Beach in Phuket, or the Bangkok bar areas seem like your cup of tea (and for a *holiday*, they are mine), I suggest that you live there first. But to do it right, you must stay for at least two or three months before you make any long-term commitments. If you can swing it, live there for at least a year. Most particularly, do not buy anything — a bar, a condo, a house, or even a motorbike. I'm going to state that again, because it is one of the most important messages of this book. *Do not buy anything right away!* Wait! After you've waited, wait some more. That once-in-a-lifetime deal on a bar is really a twice-a-week offer (and you probably don't want to be a bar owner anyway). The unbelievably cheap condo will be cheaper next month (and you probably don't really want a condo). When you buy things like this, you're stuck. Big time. Your girlfriend or your ex-pat drinking buddy may try to pressure you into making a commitment like this. Please don't. Wait. If learning how to say "no" isn't the most important thing you'll learn in Thailand, then learning how to wait is. Start from Day One. Start with the big stuff.

The best reasons for starting your new life in Thailand in one of the places I've mentioned above are many. First, you can get some idea of what it is like to live in Thailand. (It is debatable whether Pattaya, Patong Beach in Phuket and Sukhumvit Road in Bangkok are *really* Thailand, but more about that later.) You can learn some of the language. The infrastructure is good. You can make friends and meet people. You can settle down and get out of the holiday mentality. You can get used to Thai food and customs. You can learn to wait. You'll have lessons in that every day — at the bank, post office, on the road, immigration. If you don't learn the lesson of waiting, you are in deep trouble. You can learn to smile and keep a cool head.

You can learn that the women at the bars who you thought saw into your true being and really loved you, don't. They are nice, good Thai ladies, but they do not love you. You are not an exception. They have been treated well before. You are not the first nice guy they've met. If you are patient, you'll probably even meet some nice Thai ladies who aren't bar girls. You'll meet them in traditional ways — through friends, at shops or the airport.

𝓡ural 𝓣hailand

When I came to Thailand as a traveler, before I moved here, I spent some time in Northeast Thailand — called Issan.[1] I enjoyed it and before I moved here, I gave some thought to locating in Issan. As you know, at first I opted for Phuket. Now that I live in rural Issan — far from the nearest city (Udon Thani) and ten miles from the nearest town of any consequence — I realize that I probably couldn't have made it if I'd come here first. There are insurmountable language problems for one thing, and there is very little infrastructure that can be counted on, either. Even now, with my experience of living here, I doubt if I could make it on my own. I rely heavily on my Thai wife — not just because of the language, but more importantly, for friendship.

You must, however, if you live in Phuket or Pattaya or Bangkok, *visit* the real Thailand sometimes. You can do this alone, with ex-pat friends or Thai friends. That way you will slowly be exposed to the real thing and be able to make a knowledgeable decision about relocating to a less-touristed area. You may not be cut out to live, for example, in Issan. I know a lot of ex-pats who wouldn't live the way I

---

1 This word is spelled many ways: Isan, Esan, Isaan and Isarn are just a few. It is pronounced ee-sahn. See the chapter on the Thai language for more about spelling.

do for anything. In fact, when I moved, many of my friends were placing bets on how long I'd last up here. It isn't a matter of being macho. It is simply a matter of whether you can adjust to, and like, some fairly significant differences in lifestyle. And, very importantly, there is also almost a total lack of an ex-pat community for friendship, support and advice.

Houseboats in Phitsanulok, North Central Thailand.

Obviously, the two big intangible enemies for ex-pats living in rural Thailand are loneliness and boredom. You must be a fairly self-sufficient person to overcome these obstacles. Among the concrete things that can be a problem are: language, food and entertainment (books, videos, newspapers). Certainly, a place like Bangkok or Phuket has plenty of people who speak English, a lot of food from home (pizza, bread, cheese, etc.) and English-language books, videos and newspapers. In the boondocks, these things are not easily obtained. From where I live, it is a one-way trip of over two hours to find these things in any quantity. Really, if I want any sort of selection at all, I have to travel all the way to Bangkok.

Loneliness is primarily a result of lack of fluency in the Thai language. In the end, if you don't have someone who truly understands what you're talking about, life can be difficult. Sometimes you want to bounce your ideas off another person. Maybe you have a problem you want to get off your chest. We need people who speak our language and understand our culture. Out in the bush, there are not many people like that. There's no solution except to seek out fellow ex-pats. In some places there just aren't any. That requires traveling. Other than that, being a good letter writer is the only backup. Because of this, when you pick the place you want to live, you might want to consider proximity to a larger city. As I mentioned, I am two hours from Udon Thani. I'm also an hour and a half from Nong Khai, a place that has some ex-pats too. That's a help to me. You might want to be even closer to a city. Most cities of any size (Hat Yai, Kahn Kaen, Korat, etc.) have some support for ex-pats — food, entertainment, ex-pat hangouts.

One big plus relative to living in the bush is that it is amazingly cheap. You can eat for as little as 20 baht (80 cents) a day. If you can find a place to rent (there aren't many) you'll find it to be half of what you'd pay in Phuket and a third of what you'd pay in Bangkok. $80 dollars a month will rent you a nice (Thai style) house like the one where I live. Most ex-pats who live in the bush buy some land and build a house. I did that for less that $10,000. I'll write more about building a house in another chapter.

Food stall between Chiang Mai and Chiang Rai, Northern Thailand.

Many ex-pats find that alcohol is one of their biggest expenses. If you don't drink, you'll save a lot of money. If you do drink, you'll find that living in the bush, booze costs you half of what it would in a tourist destination. You can buy beer in a shop here where I live for 25 baht. In Phuket it would cost you at least 50 in a bar. If you are willing to drink Lao whiskey (not recommended), you can even drink cheaply. Slightly more, but still economical, are Mekong or Sangthip whiskey. The latter is slightly better to my taste buds.

Most Thai cities, large or small, have some entertainment in the form of "coffee shops," discos and/or karaokes. Many of these places have hostesses or singers who will sit with you. Drinking and extra-curricular activities at these establishments, when available, aren't that much cheaper than in farang establishments. It is a chance to see how things are done Thai-style, however. By the way, "coffee shops" aren't really coffee shops. They often don't have any coffee at all. Many of these entertainment places have English signs that read "Disco" or "Bar." Those that don't, frequently have large illuminated Coke or whiskey signs.

A big drawback to living in Issan or Northern Thailand is the expense and inconvenience of making your "visa runs." While Laos[2] or Cambodia or Myanmar (Burma) are nearby, visas are required to enter these countries and they are not cheap. You'll have to decide whether you want to go that route or go to Malaysia or the Philippines. If you are willing to travel to Malaysia by train or bus, you can save a lot of money. Personally, I find traveling by train to be inexpensive and comfortable and suggest that you try it. I'll talk more about visas in another chapter.

So, those are your choices — fairly touristed places with expatriate communities and infrastructure or, for lack of a better word, the real Thailand. If you remain flexible and don't make any long-term commitments, your options will remain open. Watch out

---

2 As of this writing, it is possible for me to make a visa run into Laos from Nong Khai in Thailand. From where I live, even with the expense of a Lao visa, it is cheaper than going to Malaysia. The situation with Lao visas, however, changes frequently.

for creeping procrastination, however. I write more about that in a later chapter too.

The real Thailand... rice paddies near Chiang Mai.

Chapter Four
Jobs

Perhaps you are like the vast majority of the human race and need to have some source of regular income. This chapter sketches a few ways to make money in Thailand. It is possible to do that, but for most people it is not a cakewalk. A lot of the expatriates I know have money concerns — even ones who seem like they have it made. Some have actually reached a point of desperation. Unless you have a retirement, disability income or are independently wealthy, you will have concerns too. But then, that was probably true in your home country as well.

There are many expatriates working in Thailand who are professionals or skilled workers. They teach at universities, work for oil companies, are construction engineers or lawyers. These people have gotten their jobs in their home countries or have come to Thailand and gotten lucky.

I know a teacher at a large university in Bangkok. He came to Thailand with no connections and no plans. It was his very first trip to Thailand. Within a month after he arrived, he had a professorship at the university. He receives a good salary, benefits, and has his one-year visa and work permit taken care of for him. Being a good honest Canadian, he admits that it was sheer luck. It most certainly is the exception. Other than praying, I can't tell you how to improve your odds of hitting the job jackpot.

The most common ways of earning a living in Thailand are teaching English and opening a business. In Southern Thailand, you can add being a diving instructor to the list.

Doing Business In Thailand

Thailand is like any place in regards to opening a business. It is imperative to move with caution, and to employ careful planning and thought before pursuing any business. This is true in spades in Thailand, because to you it is a foreign country and a different culture. I know many people who have gone into business and made a success of it. From travel companies to prawn farms, from bars and restaurants to souvenir shops, it is all possible. All of these business successes are extremely difficult, however, and the failure rate for small businesses in very high. Lying and cheating are more common than in the West, and the cards are stacked against you.

Bars are probably the most tempting kind of business for the average ex-pat on a budget to get involved in. I have already written about bars earlier, so I'll just remind you that my advice is *DON'T*. But, if you really want to have a bar, know what you are doing and are cut out to be a publican, my advice is this: Approach it slowly, and by no means invest your entire nest egg in a bar. I could tell you scores of tragic stories about middle-aged men who did that and lost everything. Even if you have been a bar owner in your own country, that is practically irrelevant in Thailand.

As in any country, the first trick in making a success of a business is getting customers. That is not easy if you have no friends or connections. Again, the best advice I can give is to move slowly. That way you make friends, hear about bargain rents, can wait for good deals and stand a chance of figuring out where you really are.

I know a fellow in Phuket who had been a ditch digger in Australia. He moved to Phuket after having vacationed there several times. He lived in a cheap hotel for many months, slowly looking for a bargain on a bungalow. He was also looking for a good spot to set up a small restaurant. People all over town wondered what the hell Brian was up to. They figured he should *do* something. Make a move!

Finally, when he found just what he wanted in terms of a bungalow and place for his restaurant, he did make his move. It paid off. He is making a success of things, and has even been written up in the *Bangkok Post*. But his restaurant is extremely modest, and the rent quite reasonable. He pays less than $200 a month rent and invested only a few thousand in fixtures. Had he failed, he would have lost very little.

One thing to keep in mind about setting up a business in Thailand is that foreigners cannot own real property. It is very difficult for foreigners to become Thai citizens, as well. For starters, you must first live in the country for ten years. In addition, you must be able to read, write and speak Thai. Finally, there is the bureaucracy — not fun in any country, but particularly cumbersome in Thailand. There are ways around this, of course. The most common way is to put it in a girlfriend's name. The most common *safe* way is to get a long term lease in *your* name. The second-most common safe way is to form a company. In order to do the latter, you must see a lawyer and have the appropriate legal documents drawn up. To lease a property, all you need is a lease agreement. It is up to you whether you get a lawyer involved and/or pay to have the lease translated into English. Of course, it is wise to do that.

Most leases, at least in tourist destinations like Phuket, require that you pay "key money." That is money up front for the privilege of getting the lease. It can range anywhere from a couple of thousand dollars to hundreds of thousands of dollars, depending on the length of the lease and the location of the property.

The advantages in having a lease are obvious. The main one is that it gives you an asset to sell. It also gives you security. The disadvantages are obvious, too, especially if you've paid key money. You've had to make a substantial up-front payment, and that is a commitment. Please, take your time before investing substantial capital. Make sure the lease is in *your* name — not your girlfriend's or Thai partner's.

If you have a low-key, off-the-beaten-track location for your business, you will probably have very few hassles. If you have a booming business (especially a bar), you will have a lot. One cause of hassles is bureaucracy. This is true in any country, of course, but the Thai bureaucracy is not at all what you are used to. You also have the huge liability of being unable to speak or read Thai. You are, therefore, rendered illiterate, deaf and mute in the face of a bureaucracy you know nothing about. This makes you a very dependent person, and consequently you are at risk. Assorted licenses and permits are required to do business in Thailand, and if you don't have them you are asking for trouble. The way many people get around having problems is by paying *baksheesh* (this word, of Persian derivation, means "bribe" or "gratuity," and has worked its way into Thai ex-pat lingo). From pool tables, to girls dancing naked, to staying open beyond legal operating hours, it is all possible if you pay baksheesh to the right people. This is common, but even so, it makes me nervous. I never got involved with that side of things. If you do, I suggest that you should really know what you are doing. It can easily turn into a vicious and escalating cycle. Plainly put, Thai police, in places where there is money, are corrupt. Be careful!

Another cause of difficulties in a business is labor problems. Many ex-pats haven't got a clue as to how to treat employees. When they have problems, they make sweeping, critical generalizations about Thai workers. In addition, they have expectations that reflect a double standard in relation to basic human rights. For example, they might think nothing of having their cashier work seven days a week, 10 or 12 hours a day. Moral and generous, albeit careful, business owners have far fewer labor problems than exploitative ones.

If you have a bar or restaurant or any business, and want to work in it yourself, you will need a work permit. It is possible to get one, and I know several ex-pats in Phuket and Bangkok who have them. It is a little bit expensive and time-consuming, and involves dealing with the Thai bureaucracy. There are numerous letters in the *Bangkok Post* bemoaning how difficult and time-consuming it is. Simply put, it is a hassle, and thus many ex-pats procrastinate — something that is extremely easy to do in Thailand. If you don't have a work permit, and do *anything* in your business, you are running the risk of being arrested for working illegally. It happens, and for things as minor as changing the music tape in your bar, picking up dirty dishes from a table in your restaurant or accepting money from a customer. I know scores of ex-pats who have been arrested for working. After they spend a few days or more in jail and pay a big fine and/or bribe, the first thing they do when they get out is get a work permit.

𝒯eaching 𝒥obs

Teaching English is another way of making a living in Thailand. In addition to schools at different levels, there are private language schools that hire teachers. Most hotels of any size also have a teacher or two. There are scores of other places — airlines, big business, etc.

Thai newspapers list many jobs which require fluency in English.

The two most common ways of getting teaching jobs are through ads in the English language newspapers, and by word of mouth through friends. Most of the ads in the papers are for private language schools. Some of these are legitimate operations that will even help you get your work permit and visa. Others are shoestring operations that hire you illegally. If there is a problem with your work permit, it is you who will be arrested. This doesn't happen often, but it does happen. Pay at private language schools, as well as public schools operated by the Thai government, is usually quite low. In Phuket, for example, it is 100 to 125 baht an hour. A little arithmetic will show you that you have to teach a lot of hours to make a living at that rate. In Bangkok the pay is higher, but so is the cost of living.

Teaching jobs in hotels are usually gotten via connections, although beating the bushes can land you a job at a hotel. Hotel jobs pay better (20,000 — 35,000 baht a month), and usually provide other benefits, such as accommodations, visa, work permit and often times food. Three-star hotels in major tourist areas are the spots to check for these kinds of jobs. Living in a place and making friends and contacts are the best ways of acquiring a job at a hotel. Making the rounds and asking to speak to the hotel's training manager often-times pays off as well.

Many people wonder about credentials. Most jobs require a Bachelor's Degree, and normally it doesn't matter what the degree is in. More and more jobs are requiring English-as-a-Second-Language (ESL) certification. Some jobs only require that you are a native speaker of English. The fact of the matter is that many English teachers — especially at private language schools and hotels — acquired their jobs using phony credentials. This is easy to do, since usually only a photocopy of a college degree is required to "prove" that you have one. That makes changing the name on the degree quite simple. I know two English teachers at big hotels who acquired their jobs with forged degrees. One, who never even graduated from high school, went on to become the training manager. I don't recommend this way of doing things, and I leave it up to you to answer the moral question involved. I will say, however, that if you have solid, real credentials, you improve your chances of getting a good teaching job.

Universities are much more careful about credentials, and will probably check.

If you have a Master's Degree or Ph.D. in almost any discipline or you have real ESL credentials, there is a good chance of landing a job in academia. Often times, only a B.A. is required. The best way to do this is to go to Thailand, keep your eye on the help-wanted ads, and make the rounds. Legitimate jobs in academia pay up to $2,000 a month, and take care of your work permit and visa for you. Some offer health insurance. If you are "over-educated" in the States, or find that no one wants to employ someone with a Master's Degree in, say, English or History, Thailand is the place for you.

Thai schools' and universities' school year runs from June to mid-October, and from November to mid-March. Come to Thailand a month before a semester begins. Bring your degrees, transcripts, certificates and letters of reference. Check the *Bangkok Post* daily (especially Saturday), and you will almost certainly land a job.

𝒟iving 𝒥obs

Let me add just a word about being a diving instructor, since it is a common form of employment in Southern Thailand. While I know nothing about diving, I do have several friends who are instructors. It would, of course, be foolish to forge credentials in this department. If you are a diver yourself, and don't have instructor's credentials, you can take a course and become an instructor. That's a good way of meeting people and perhaps getting a job. Other than that, the best thing to do is to go to one of the major diving destinations (Phuket and Ko Samui are the biggest), hang around and get to know the local diving community. Pay for divers can be reasonable, and as with nearly everything in Thailand, the longer you stay, the busier you will be.

As with any employment in Thailand, a work permit is required. Some elect to chance it and not get one. Again, this is not recommended.

Except for those who work for major international corporations, most ex-pats acquire their jobs in-country. As mentioned, the

Bangkok Post has a large help-wanted section on Saturdays. As is the case in most countries, the ads are dominated by companies looking for technical experts in fields such as engineering, electronics, pharmaceuticals and the like. There are always a number of ads for English teachers, as well. As far as finding work in Thailand goes, there is no substitute for being in-country.

Todd was from America, and he'd come into some money as a result of an accident he'd had at work. It was a fair chunk of change — maybe 2 million baht ($80,000). He decided he was going to go to Thailand and set up a business. I first met him as a customer in my bar in Phuket.

His business idea was to export fancy Thai clothes for women. He claimed to have contacts all over the States and Canada. He talked about exporting hand-painted silk blouses and selling Thai-style dresses to businesses all over the world. He talked about it a lot. That's all he did, for months, every day.

Also every day, he drank — making the rounds of his favorite watering holes, spending 5 to 10,000 baht on booze, and occasionally women, daily, without fail. He did nothing about his clothing idea for months. One day he showed up at my home to announce a new plan. He was going to open a language school and travel agency. His conversation changed from clothing to schooling. His routine, however, remained the same. Stay out every night until 5 or 6 AM, get roaring drunk and then go to bed. He'd wake up only 2 or 3 hours later and do his laundry by hand in the name of saving money. He told all his friends how early he woke up and how busy he was. But every day, he'd go back to bed about 6 in the evening and sleep for 4 or 5 more hours. He'd wake up depressed and uncommunicative, and sometimes he'd watch a video on his rented set. Then, somewhere between midnight and 2 AM, he'd go out again. Drinking.

His life grew moderately saner when he hooked up with a woman named Phen who moved in with him. He claimed he didn't really love her because he knew she was a bar girl. Instead of going out drinking late in the evening, he began going out about 9. He didn't drink as much but he spent just as much, because he was buying drinks and food for Phen.

Todd fell hard for a bar girl. Was this the one?

After Phen and Todd were together for a couple of months, he came to me and said that he had learned that Phen already had a boy friend — a man from Switzerland who had sent her 10,000 baht a month for 2 years and who only came to Thailand on holiday for two weeks every year. She wanted to know if Todd would mind her spending two weeks with the Swiss man and, after that, return to Todd. He said he didn't mind, but it obviously drove him crazy.

Two days after Phen moved out to stay in a fancy hotel with her Swiss boyfriend, she returned to Todd, saying she didn't like the other guy any more and was finished with him. Todd was ecstatic. Phen stayed for two days, and then told Todd that she wanted to go to her bungalow, which she had never given up, and pick up some items of clothing. She didn't return that day, or the next. Todd was at his wits' end. He asked me if I would go on a walkabout with him to look for her. Since he seemed almost suicidal, I agreed.

We found her at her old bar — an open air "beer bar" tucked in among 20 others just like it. We didn't approach her, but sat at another bar and watched to see what happened. She appeared not to notice us, but you never know. She laughed and joked and touched and even kissed the guy she was sitting with — the Swiss man, we assumed.

Todd got drunker and drunker, and finally Phen left with the man and still Todd drank on. The only hope for him not getting into a lot of trouble was to line him up with a woman. Finally I did — two women, actually. Sisters. Honest-to-goodness sisters, not just bar girl sisters.

Three days later, Phen came back to Todd. He asked her about the Swiss man, and Phen said she was finished with him. He told her what he had seen, and she claimed that it was not the Swiss man he had seen her with, but rather just a friend. Phen moved back in with Todd.

For three days.

Then, she disappeared for a week. Todd, in spite of himself, began asking around about her. Word on the bamboo telegraph was that Phen had gone to Bangkok to get a passport and visa to go to Switzerland.

When she returned again, she went to see Todd who asked her where she had been. "I go home see Mama. Very sick," was her reply. Todd knew better than to believe that, but he did anyway. Back in she moved.

For a week.

Then she disappeared. Todd never saw her again. Neither did I. I hope she likes the cold winters in Switzerland.

Todd pissed the rest of his money away. But he did manage to scrounge up 3,000 baht to buy some women's clothes from an Indian tailor. "Samples," he called them. Nearly in tears he said good-bye to return to the States. He claimed he'd be back within a year, but he never returned. I did get a letter from him once. He said he made the rounds with his samples, and that the same thing could be purchased in retail shops for less than he could sell it for. He said he was unemployed and broke and living with his mother. He asked me if there were any English teaching jobs around. He asked if I'd seen Phen.

I didn't write back to him. I didn't see the point.

Chapter Five
Visas

We are foreigners in Thailand; not just culturally, but legally as well. Thailand is quite generous about letting foreigners visit their country, and even allows them to stay for a long period of time. As with any country, however, you must jump through certain hoops. We may not enjoy the hoops, but jump we must.

I am not an expert on Thai immigration law, and things change. This is a brief description of what I do know and what is the case as of this writing. If something is very important to you, go directly to Thai Immigration and ask. In spite of criticism from many fault-finding farangs, I have found Immigration officials to be helpful. They are certainly more gracious than their Western counterparts. Fellow ex-pats are usually up-to-date on the situation with visas as well.

There are four ways to enter Thailand and stay for varying periods of time.

One-Year Visa

Those with work permits or people who can document that they have sufficient incomes can get a one-year visa. For those wanting to live in Thailand, this is the best way to go. Unless you get a job where the visa is taken care of for you, there is some disagreement among ex-pats as to the best way to get a one-year visa. It is somewhat of a mysterious black hole, and the best way to proceed is to bite the bullet and go to Immigration and find out for yourself. Remember to be patient and polite, no matter how frustrated you may get. Aside from that, some lawyers and other agencies claim to be able to assist in acquiring a one-year visa.

Non-Immigrant Visa[1]

A non-immigrant visa allows you to stay in the country for 90 days. After that, even if you have a double-entry or triple-entry visa, you still must leave the country. For example, if you have a double-entry non-immigrant visa, you can stay for 90 days. After 90 days, you must go to (say) Malaysia. You get stamped out of Thailand; then, after staying in Malaysia for one minute or longer, you re-enter Thailand. That gives you 90 more days in the country. After that period, because you had a double-entry visa, you must leave again, but this time get a new visa. Some people get triple-entry visas.

In order to get a non-immigrant visa, you must provide a Thai Consulate with two passport-size photos of yourself and a letter stating that you are doing business in Thailand or that you are a student (perhaps at a language school). The business letter should not, of course, say that you are working in Thailand, because, without a work permit, that is illegal.

A sample of a business letter is on page 43.

Most people get their initial visa in their home country. (You cannot get a visa in Thailand itself. It must be acquired from a Thai consulate outside of the country.) I suggest you try to get a triple-entry non-immigrant visa.

---

1 In Feb. of 1995, the Thai Government made it technically possible to obtain visas and get extensions without leaving the country. The bureaucracy is so cumbersome and the functionaries so uncertain, however, that as of this writing 99.9 per cent of ex-pats are doing things the "old way." That way is described in this section.

Dear Sir or Madam,

As a manufacturer of ladies garments here in New Zealand, we have asked that Mr. Jim Smith (N.Z. passport number 12345678) purchase Thai silk and cotton for export. We therefore respectfully request that you grant him a double-entry, non-immigrant visa.

Sincerely,

Robert Jones
President

Many people do their "turn-arounds" (exit/re-entry) in Malaysia. They either go to Hat Yai in Southern Thailand and then take a taxi or bus to the Malaysian border, or they fly to Penang in Malaysia, oftentimes returning on the same day.

Penang is also a popular destination for getting new visas. The big drawback to going there is that many ex-pats have had difficulty getting a multiple-entry visa. It seems to be less of a problem getting a multiple-entry visa in the Philippines, and, by the time all is said and done, it isn't that much more expensive to go there. Neither have I had a problem getting a multiple- (triple-) entry visa in the States.

The main reason many ex-pats choose Malaysia is that it is nearby, and no visa is required to enter the country. The Philippines doesn't require a visa either. Laos, Myanmar (Burma), Cambodia and Vietnam all require visas to enter their territory, and these visas along with transportation and accommodations are not, as of this writing, as economical as going to Malaysia.

Be sure to check the date your *visa* expires — especially if you have a multiple-entry visa. I got my first double-entry visa in the U.S. before moving to Thailand. It was good for 180 days — which makes sense, because it was a double-entry visa. The next double-entry visa I got was from the Philippines. I received the visa and stayed in Angeles City for about a week before returning to Thailand. I checked to make sure the visa was a double-entry, but I did not check to see how long it was good for. 90 days after I returned to Thailand, I went to Hat Yai for my turn-around, only to discover that my visa had expired. They'd made it good for only 90 days. I got my automatic two-weeks stay,[2] but had to fly to Penang to get another visa. Don't let this happen to you. For instance, if your visa itself expires on January 15, you must make your (last) entry into the country *before* that date — i.e., January 14 or earlier. This is something to keep in mind particularly with triple-entry visas (which are valid for only six months). For example, if you get a triple-entry visa on December 1, the *visa* expires on the following June 1. During the six-month interim, you must leave the country on a turn-around two times, but you do not need to get another visa. When you re-enter, you have another three months, but you must make your final entries before June 1. After you have used your three entries within the allotted six months, you must obtain a new visa. Also, you should not apply for your visa too early. The visa is good for six months (maximum) from the date of issue — *not* from the date of your first entry into the country.

The best reason for getting a non-immigrant visa is that it allows you to stay in Thailand without going to Immigration for an extension. (Non-immigrant visas cannot, under most circumstances, be extended.) It also allows you certain legal privileges, such as buying a car or motorbike and putting it in your name. In addition, it is easier to get a work permit if you have a non-immigrant visa. If you have merely a tourist visa, you will have to leave the country, get a non-immigrant visa, return and then apply for the work permit.

Tourist Visa

A tourist visa lets you stay in the country for 60 days, but it can be extended for 30 days by going to the nearest Immigration office. Tourist visas are much easier to obtain than non-immigrant visas. There is really nothing wrong with a tourist visa, provided you don't want to own a motor vehicle or get a work permit, and there is an Immigration office near you.

---

2 One change that *has* been instituted is that Americans and most others now get an automatic 30-day stay in the country without needing a visa.

Visa Services

I have heard stories of people who pay well-connected individuals to obtain their visa or "do" their turnaround for them. Personally, it makes me nervous to be without my passport, and the legality of this is questionable in my mind. I don't worry about laws per se, but I wouldn't like to spend time in a Thai jail or be deported.

Popular "visa destinations" such as Penang in Malaysia or Manila and Angeles City in the Philippines have visa services — oftentimes at hotels or travel agencies — that will do all the running around and waiting for you. It is worth the small expense.

Most people don't enjoy dealing with Immigration and there are frequent letters in the *Bangkok Post* complaining. I'm not crazy about leaving Thailand every three months and having to deal with bureaucrats either. But I try to keep in mind how very difficult it is for Thai people to go to America (or England or Australia), and how even Americans are treated upon returning to their *own* country. By comparison, Thai Immigration is polite and helpful indeed. No matter what your feelings are on this issue, though, always — but *ALWAYS* — be affable and cordial with Immigration officials. It is also wise to dress "decently" when going to Immigration. See Chapter Seventeen, "Final Thoughts," for some examples of what *not* to wear.

As mentioned above, some countries make it extremely difficult for Thais to obtain even a tourist visa. This is particularly true if the Thai is a young, unmarried woman. Keep this in mind before making promises to your darling about a trip home with you.

Those countries which are reasonable relative to Thais entering their country, Thailand is reasonable in return. People from Norway, Sweden, Finland and New Zealand can come to Thailand and stay for 90 days without any visa whatsoever. If you want to put pressure on anyone, it seems to me that pressuring your own government to relax its visa restrictions for Thai people is the way to go.

One thing to remember when determining where you want to live is how convenient getting a visa is. Obviously, living in Hat Yai makes things much easier than living in Bangkok, or especially

Northern Thailand. Phuket isn't bad, either. Even taking the bus from Phuket to Hat Yai is not too much of a hassle, as the trip is only seven hours. One of the reasons I chose to live in Phuket when I first moved to Thailand was its proximity to the Malaysian border.

You don't have to be an anarchist to long for a world without visas. Without passports. There certainly is something absurd about having to leave a country for a few minutes, merely for the sake of leaving and having some functionaries rubber-stamp your passport. Unfortunately, a world without passports seems to be a long ways away. For the moment, all we can do is try to look on the bright side of things. A "visa run" is an excuse to get away, have a break in our routine, and see some of the world. Living in the bush, as I do now, it offers an opportunity to see civilization again, to stock up on books and farang food, to speak English. For bar owners in Phuket or Bangkok, it is a chance to rest from the grind.

Racism, xenophobia, power, fear and greed are the primary reasons for passports and visas. Most Western countries have serious cases of these problems. We should do the best we can to fight these evils. That means, among other things, being tolerant and open-minded of other cultures and world-views. It means setting a good example by being a good farang.

Jim was a retired Master Chief in the U.S. Navy. He'd been to Phuket many times while in the Navy, and after retiring he decided to move there and make it his home. He had been divorced from his wife for many years, and had a grown daughter. His money and his life were his own, and he lived life to its fullest. He was an absolute character: crotchety but friendly and generous and helpful. He was a teetotaler who made the rounds of the bars nearly every night, drinking Coke or coffee or orange juice but buying drinks for friends and ladies alike.

When Jim heard that a Navy ship was pulling into Phuket, he always went to the Shore Patrol office and gave them a letter to hand over to the ship's Command Master Chief. Here is what it said:

Fr: Jim Grimes, HMCM/USN (Ret.)
To: Command Master Chief
Subj: Fun in the Sun

    1. As you can tell from the heading, I'm a retired dick smith and porthole checker.[3] I retired as CMC, USNH Long Beach, CA., 25 Jan 92. I arrived here on 21 Apr 92 and have not had a bad day since.

    2. There are 4 reasons why I am a happy man:

        a. I have no business to give me a headache

        b. I have no motorbike to give me a body ache

        c. I have no permanent girlfriend or wife to give me a pain in the ass.

        d. I get an alimony[4] from Cleveland every month.

I live very, very comfortably here on $1600/mo which is not my full retirement pay. I have a 3 bedroom house, maid, laundry service and am out and about almost every night. This also includes trips for a vacation from my vacation every 3 months.[5]

    3. I write this letter to offer you or your crew any assistance I can possibly provide. I have no need to talk Navy, old or new, since I now talk Phuket, Patong. Basically, I know the island. I have no one place to push. I know the restaurants, bars and girls I like. Some you will find on your own. Others are off the beaten track. You will have fun no matter whether you run into me or not.

    4. I am enclosing a rough map of some of my regular haunts. I usually don't start out until about 20:30. All of the places have cold beer and hot women. If I see you, I will buy you a toddy for your body in appreciation to you for protecting my ass while I'm getting my ass. If I don't see you, fair winds and following seas.

    Very respectfully,

Jim Grimes

Jim said about half the time he hooked up with some of the sailors from a ship and usually had a good time with them. He was just that kind of guy. He loved Thailand and had no time for ex-pats who were cynical or nasty about their adopted country. He avoided the bars with burned-out, negative owners who did nothing but complain. If you were to see him on his nightly rounds, or out on an errand during the day, and asked him how he was, he never failed to say — "Good. Every day, very good." If a Thai person asked him how he was, he responded the same way in Thai.

---

3 Navy slang for hospital corpsman.
4 Retirement pay.
5 "Visa run."

In the months before I moved from Phuket, I began to notice that Jim seemed moody and grouchy. He didn't go out as much. When I stopped over to his house, he was uncommonly silent. One day I came right out and asked him if he was *really* OK. He insisted that he was. But I worried about him.

I said good-bye to Jim and the rest of Phuket on Oct. 5, 1994. I wrote Jim a letter a month or two after I got settled in my new home. No reply came. Then, one day I got a letter from Jim's daughter who was in Phuket. She told me that Jim had been found unconscious on his bathroom floor by one of his two housekeepers. He'd had a stroke, and she'd flown in from Iowa to take care of him. Jim had always been as kind and helpful and generous to his housekeepers as he was to all Thais and farangs alike. Now, these two wonderful women repaid his kindness by staying at his hospital bed 24 hours a day for three weeks until he was med-evacked home.

A couple of months later I got another letter from Jim's daughter. Jim had died of cancer and assorted other maladies. He'll be missed by all of his friends in Thailand — lawyers and tuk-tuk drivers, bar owners and bar girls, shopkeepers and doctors, friends and neighbors. I can think of no finer example of how to be a good ex-pat — a good farang — than Jim.

Chapter Six
Costs

There's no such thing as a free lunch. True enough. But Thailand has something for everyone in every price range. The rich have ample opportunities to spend their money in Thailand. The good news is that those who aren't independently wealthy can live nicely on a budget — if they are willing to be flexible. Most particularly, if they are willing to do things Thai-style.

From the early days of tourism in Thailand, when backpackers were greeted with open arms, Thai people have both welcomed and understood those who must be economical. Old-timers and hardened tourists will tell you that it isn't the same as it used to be. The fact is, nothing on earth is the same as it was 15 minutes ago, never mind 20 years ago. But, if you must be careful with your money, like most people, there is a place for you in the land of smiles. Don't listen to the cynics.

The cost of living in Thailand can be summarized as follows: Thai food and Thai-style housing are cheap. Foreign food is expensive. First-class housing is on par with the West. Alcohol — especially beer and imported whiskey — is expensive. Transportation by bus and train or your own motorbike is very reasonable. Transportation by air is slightly cheaper than the West.

Keeping in mind these generalizations and the fact that things change, let me be more specific and give some examples.

ᕼousing

The author's home in Northern Thailand.

Obviously, housing in Bangkok is more expensive than in, say, Issan. Still, if you are willing to live in a single room, you can obtain accommodations in Bangkok for as little as 3,500 baht a month. I doubt if you'd be happy, however. A more reasonable expectation is 5 to 8,000 baht (about 2 to 3 hundred dollars) a month. 10-11,000 baht (approximately $400) would do quite nicely. Another factor, when considering Bangkok, is which part of the city you're talking about. If you live well out of any of the city's centers — near the airport, for instance — you can rent a nice apartment for 8 to 10 thousand. Of course, if you live well out of the city proper, you're dealing with one of the worst traffic situations in the world — meaning commutes into town that take an hour or more each way.

If you want to live in Bangkok, I suggest asking moderately priced hotels what their monthly rates are, while you look for a proper apartment. This will give you time to meet people who might know of something. It will also give you a chance to check the *Bangkok Post* and *The Nation* where, occasionally, moderately-priced accommodations are listed.

Phuket is somewhat more economical than Bangkok. This is largely because of over-development. It's a renter's market there — especially in the off-season. When I lived there, I stayed in three different places. One was a one-bedroom furnished apartment with a kitchen and a refrigerator, a bathroom and a small living room. It cost me 3,500 baht ($140) a month. The second place was a two-bedroom furnished apartment similar to the first, and it cost 4,500 baht ($180) a month. The last, and best, place was a furnished three-bedroom Thai-style house that cost me 5,500 baht ($220) a month, with the electric included. I usually had one of the bedrooms rented out for about 2,000 baht ($80) a month. Before I moved into a bungalow, I stayed in a hotel where I received a discount for long-term residents — it cost me 4,000 baht ($160) a month.

Many people with a bit of money are tempted by condos. Unfortunately, as with bar owners, I have met very few happy condo owners. Sam is a typical case. After retiring, he moved with his wife to Phuket and spent over 2 million baht ($80,000) on a condo. From the day he moved in he was frustrated and angry with the hidden costs for services, poor maintenance and general lack of interest the management had in its residents. After living in the condo for a month, he put it up for sale. Two years later, he is still living there and still trying to sell it. Given the low rents for bungalows, two million baht would have gone a long way. Even in Phuket, with its high real estate prices, Sam could have bought a decent house for the money he spent on the condo.

As mentioned elsewhere in this book, foreigners cannot own real property. There are ways around this. Long-term leases and forming a company are the two most common. Check with a lawyer, but make sure he's a reliable one. Foreigners can own a condo.

Electricity

Electricity bills vary a lot. If you don't have air conditioning your electric bill should be somewhere between 200 and 500 baht ($8-$10) a month. If it is much more than 500 baht, something is wrong. With the exception of Bangkok, I would not recommend having air conditioning. Most people can get used to merely using a fan. They're cheaper, and better for your health. Even here in Issan, where the hot season is as bad as it is anywhere, a fan is adequate for me.

There is one thing to be careful about. Some landlords inflate the price of electric bills. Find out if you pay the bill to the electric company yourself, or if the landlord reads the meter and gives you the bill. If it is the latter, you may be getting ripped off. He may be doing the same thing with the water and phone bill.

Food

Even in Bangkok or Phuket, Thais can live on as little as 20 to 40 baht (less than $2) a day for food. You can too, if you're willing to eat Thai food exclusively. Most ex-pats need an occasional, if not frequent, dose of food from home. Things like cheese, potatoes and beef are relatively expensive. The more you crave food from home, the greater your food budget is going to be.

Eating Thai food at food stalls is a fairly inexpensive proposition, so it isn't essential to have a kitchen in your home. Again, eating farang food in a restaurant is relatively expensive.

I like my dose of farang food, but I am a vegetarian, so my food budget might be a bit less than most farangs'. Also, for some time now, I have lived in a home with a kitchen, and I rarely eat out. That *is* an advantage with farang food. I suppose I spend about 30 to 50 baht ($2) a day on food for myself. In Bangkok, as well as at tourist destinations, many ingredients for cooking your own farang food are available.[1]

Food stall cook, in Phrae.

---

1 Many farangs use visa runs to Penang to stock up on food from home. It is cheaper, and there is a wider selection.

While much of it is expensive, it is certainly cheaper than eating out.

Alcohol and Entertainment

For many ex-pats, the biggest expense is booze. You don't have to be an alcoholic, either. If you buy Thai beer by the case to take home, it costs about 500 baht. That's a tad over 20 baht (80 cents) a beer. Imported whiskey, purchased at a shop and drunk at home, is a bit more reasonable. A bottle of gin or vodka is about 300 baht ($12). Drinking Thai-style is much cheaper. A bottle of Mekong is about 100 baht ($4), and Sangthip about 110 baht. Lao whiskey is only 45 baht ($1.80) a bottle. I am not a whiskey drinker, but I suggest that if you want to drink Thai whiskey, you make it Sangthip. It is not as raw, and causes fewer problems the next day. All Thai whiskey is fairly notorious for causing weird dreams. You can deduce what this indicates about its ingredients. By the same token, regular Singha beer is quite potent, and often results in hangovers. Try Singha Gold or Singha Draft. Other beers brewed in Thailand are Amarit, Kloster and Carlsberg. These are a bit more expensive than Singha brands.

Drinking in bars is, by Thai standards, very expensive. Beer is about 50 baht ($2) a bottle, mixed drinks 60 baht or more apiece. If you're in a holiday center such as Phuket, you'll have other expenses. Odds are you'll end up buying other people drinks (especially ladies), and perhaps acquiring a companion for the night. My suggestion for buying ladies drinks is that you don't go overboard, and that you say something like, "Can I buy you a beer? or gin and tonic? or Mekong Coke?" If you simply say, "Can I buy you a drink?" it just might end up being an expensive cocktail or premium whiskey. Most places in Bangkok have what they call "lady drinks," which run from 40 to 70 baht each, depending on where you are.

If you have a big night on the town, buy a few drinks for others and take a companion for the night, you should be able to do that for as little as 1,500 to 2,000 baht ($60-$80) for the evening. You're spending too much if it costs more than that. In addition, if you do that everyday, your budget will be in serious straits — and believe me, it is easy to do it every day. I know scores of ex-pats who have gone to Thailand with thousands or even tens of thousands of dollars in their pockets. Their intentions were to live and work here. After a year or two of procrastinating and drinking and shagging women every night, they returned home with nothing.

Buying Land and Building a House

After you have made a long-term lease agreement or set up a company, you may then want to build a house. I know of no one who has done this on their own. Everyone I know has done this in conjunction with their Thai wife. It is therefore imperative that you have someone you can trust. I'm not an advice columnist, but I strongly suggest you live with your lady for at least a year before making a commitment for land and a house. I do not mean know her for one year while you come and go from Thailand and probably deposit money into her bank account. I mean live with her on a day-to-day basis for a year. Most of the horror stories you hear are true. I could relate a lot of them myself. Believe me, every one of the guys who tells you their tragic tale thought that they were the exception, and that their woman was different and special. If you aren't sure and careful you will, at the very least, end up miserable. In addition to that, you may end up broke. While I am in no position to judge the women involved, I can say that most of these tragic tales concern a farang who acted stupidly.

In addition to that, take the necessary legal steps to protect yourself. Do this no matter how much you trust your partner in life. People and situations change. It is best if "power" is evenly distributed. My wife owns our land and house. I have a lease from her for 30 years, renewable for 30 more. Another friend of mine drew up an agreement that says his wife owns the land, but he owns the house and everything in it. I suggest these legal maneuvers not out of paranoia or distrust, but rather because having a clear-cut agreement can help prevent, or at least minimize, problems. Don't be immature, and don't be lazy. If it is worth doing, it is worth doing *right!*

Buying land and building a house in big cities and tourist destinations is comparable to doing so in the United States. You're talking about $100,000 (U.S.) or more.

In rural Thailand, things are different. I bought land and built a house with a shop front in Northeast Thailand. The land (about half an acre) cost me $700. It already had a well, and plenty of fruit trees. My modest one-story, 4-room house cost me less than $8,000 to build. It has many Western amenities — running water, windows, ceiling, etc. If you truly felt you could live Thai-style, you could get by for *much* less than I did. Regardless of which route you go, one giant benefit is that you have no rent or mortgage payments at all. That is very liberating. (Owners of real property must pay a small tax to the district office. In most cases, that amounts to well under $100 a year. Income taxes, for ex-pats, are deducted from their salaries if they are working legally. Those taxes amount to about 10% of their salaries. Those ex-pats who are working illegally pay no income taxes, of course.)

When you look for someone to build your house, do not go by price alone. Ask to see other houses the person has constructed. In addition to that, make sure you are physically at the building site every day to make sure things are done properly. In my case, I chose the person who had the *highest* "bid" for the work, because it was clear that he knew what he was doing. Do not get things all set up for construction and then go back to work or hang out in Bangkok while the work takes place. Big mistake! You must be at the building site every day. Mistakes — some of them outrageous — are 100% certain if you aren't.

My house is made primarily of cement. Wood in Thailand is quite expensive. If, however, you must have a wooden house, you can buy a Thai-style house, take it apart and move it to your land for less than $4,000.

Chapter Seven
Thai Women

Thai women are among the most beautiful and helpful in the world. They are enchanting. They are magic. Consequently, you should beware.

This chapter is quite obviously written by a man and aimed at men. In addition, it is written for those adventurers who come to Thailand without connections or friends in "respectable" or mainstream positions. Plainly put, it is written for those who, initially at least, will not have the opportunity to meet professional or traditional Thai women.

I feel quite certain that most ex-pats in Thailand are men. There are women ex-pats, of course, and I know a couple. One even lives up here in the bush in a nearby town and has a Thai boyfriend. But there is no way I can speak for, or even about, the experiences of women ex-pats. Some things I have written about in this book — jobs, business, visa — of course are applicable to women as well as men. But there are some things that a man experiences here, relative to Thai women, that are rather unique.

People come to Thailand for many reasons. The weather is (for most of the year) lovely — at least for those who don't mind heat and humidity. Thai people are terrific. They generally have an open-minded and live-and-let-live approach to life. The lifestyle is easy-going and laid-back. Buddhism is a wonderful and tolerant religion. Politically, in spite of what you may read or hear, Thailand is a very stable place. This is due to the fact that the King and the rest of the

Royal Family are loved, respected and heeded — and deservedly so, for they are absolutely wonderful people. They have essentially no legal power. The power that they have is moral. That is evidenced by the fact that Thailand is the only remaining Buddhist monarchy on the planet.

Hill tribe girls near the Burmese border.

These are some of the reasons people are attracted to Thailand. There are many others. The fact of the matter is, however, that most men come to Thailand primarily because of Thai women. I am not saying that is the *only* reason they come, but it is a *big* reason they come. It certainly had something to do with my coming here, and most of my friends admit it as well.

Unless you are a professional type, odds are that the first woman who will engage your attention will be a bar girl or go-go dancer. This is true even though women in these and related occupations constitute, at most, 1% of the population. In Bangkok you will find them in the Nana Entertainment Complex on Soi 4 off Sukhumvit Road, and at Soi Cowboy which runs between Sois 21 and 23 off Sukhumvit. You will also find "lady bars" in Patpong in Bangkok, Patong Beach in Phuket, and Pattaya. Chiang Mai has a few, but not many. Many male vacationers come to Thailand for the sole purpose of visiting these places. Call them "sex tourists" if you want to. Most men I know who fall into that category think it's funny and joke about it.

The Western media has frequently painted unfair and derogatory pictures of the "sex business" in Thailand. It is offensive to Thai people and it is offensive to me. The primary reasons for these grossly exaggerated reports are sensationalism, political correctness or both. Don't believe them. Please.

I hesitate to call the women (mostly young) who work at these establishments prostitutes. I refuse to call them whores. The job that these women do has no counterpart in the West. Yes, they sell their bodies. But, generally speaking, they will not go with just any man, and the fact is that they approach their work, as nearly all Thais do, with a sense of fun. Plainly put, these women are different than any you have met in the West.

Since we are talking about a rather large number of people — hundreds of thousands by conservative estimates — it is impossible to generalize about what kind of human beings bar girls are. There are friendly ones with good attitudes and grouchy ones with bad attitudes. If I were to generalize, however, here are some of the things I would conclude.

These bar girls came from rural villages.

Most of these women come from poor rural villages — oftentimes in Northeast Thailand. Some of them are illiterate, and few have gone beyond the sixth grade in school. Sometimes their family knows what work they are doing (but choose to ignore it), but often they don't. There is, at the end of the day, a choice involved in the career that these women have selected. They could have stayed in their villages and worked rice. They could have left their village and worked in hotels, restaurants or construction. Most Thai women, of course, choose one of these options or other "respectable" work. The problem is that none of these jobs offers much in the way of remuneration — especially for someone with no education. Working in a bar, even for the average-looking Thai woman, offers the chance of making decent money. If they make decent money, they can then take better care of their families, and this is of primary importance. I'm not saying that all these women follow through on helping their families out, but most do, and it is the most common explanation you will hear as to why they do what they do. It is always a variation on this theme: "I have to work bar to help Mama and Papa because they have no money." "I work bar to buy milk for my baby." Fairly early on in your encounter with a bar girl, you will hear something along these lines. I guarantee it.

The job of a bar girl entails some of the following as part of its job description: Must be happy and friendly and get customers to drink more. Must get the customer to buy "lady drinks" for which the bar girl gets a commission. After getting the customer to spend a lot of money at the bar, must get the customer to pay the "bar fine" so that the bar girl can sleep with him. Lady gets a commission on the bar fine. The customer will pay the lady anywhere from 500 baht ($20) up — the morning after. Then, if the lady is lucky, she can get the customer to take her shopping — preferably for gold, but clothes will do. And don't worry about eating; the customer will pay for all the food, maybe at an expensive restaurant. The good bar girl gets the customer to come back to her bar again and again. The bad one pisses off with the customer and goes bar-hopping and discoing all over town. Bar owners aren't real fond of that, even though they are getting a portion of the daily bar fine — which is paid because the bar is missing one of its primary assets: a woman.

In exchange for paying the bar and the woman, the customer will get taken care of. Old-timers say that the ladies don't take care of customers like they did in the good old days. Probably true. And that they are spoiled and want too much of everything. Probably true. But the fact of the matter is, even a mediocre bar girl will take care of her customer like he has never, in this age of women's liberation, been taken care of before. The first time a Western male comes here, he thinks he's died and gone to male heaven. He looks like it, too, because of the stars in his eyes. When and if reality sets in is another matter. If the man is in Thailand on vacation and has a hefty holiday budget, it doesn't matter if reality reaches him or not. If the man lives in Thailand or is looking for his dream girl, well, that's another matter.

What is reality? Hopefully, the man isn't so lonely that his primary motive for being here is to find the woman of his dreams. That can lead to disaster, both emotionally and financially. Let's assume that we're talking about a reasonably mature, reasonably intelligent man who will not marry a bar girl in the space of two weeks, who will not return to the West and send hundreds of dollars to her every month and expect her to stay away from the bar life, who will not deplete every asset he has at home and move to Thailand and build a house for her and the entire family and put it in her name. Let's assume we're talking about a man with a degree of common sense who can withstand the huge temptation to do any or all of the above. And believe me, it is a temptation.

Reality is that this woman has a job, and she is doing it for money. She does not love you. She might like you, as your local bookseller or postal employee does, but she does not *love* you. Your local bookseller isn't going to give you free books, but she is going to like you more if you're a good customer. No doubt, she'll even do extras for you. But that's her job. She's a professional bookseller. You're not her only customer, and you're not her only friend. You're not the only one who is kind and polite to her.

Reality is that you don't love this woman even though you might think you do. You know nothing about her — how can you, when you've only known her for two weeks? You don't know where she comes from. Oh, sure, you've both done the routine "Where you come from?" questions, but I'm talking about where she *really* comes from. And she doesn't know where you come from, even though you told her that you're American or English or German. To emphasize this, show her a map of the world. You shouldn't be surprised when she is unable to locate the U.S.A. But ask her where Thailand is. Odds are 100 to 1 that she won't be able to find her own country on the map. That doesn't mean she is stupid. It means that she is uneducated, and that is one of many huge obstacles that lie between you and her.

Reality is that she comes from a village where there is a lifestyle you can't imagine unless you've been there. Lucky families have electricity and an outside toilet. Virtually no one has a phone, car, motorbike, stove, furniture, inside running water and other assorted whatnots. Your daily booze budget would do them nicely for a week. If you visit her village with her, you will think that it is quaint and you will want to help. It is not quaint (it is reality), and any help you provide should wait a spell and be done in moderation. If you visit her village you will be expected to pay for a lot of things — particularly food and booze. That's OK within reason. You will also be expected to give some money to Mama and Papa. That's OK too — within reason. It is important that you visit your girlfriend's village, but you should wait awhile before you do it. It sends strong messages about your intentions, and it puts assorted pressures on you as well as on her. Wait!

Here are a few random thoughts pertaining to Thai women.

First, put one myth out of your mind. Prostitution was not invented by American GIs on R and R from the Vietnam War. Certainly, the go-go format was the result of Thai adaptability and entrepreneurship. But Thai-style nightery entertainment predates the Vietnam War by decades, if not centuries.

If 1% of Thai women work in the world's oldest profession, then 99% don't. It is possible to meet women who engage in more "respectable" occupations, but it takes time. Perhaps more time than it does in the West. Traditional Thai ladies are often modest and even shy. Odds are that the first time you go out with one you will be "chaperoned" by one of her friends. Public displays of affection, even hand-holding, are not practiced — even by married couples.

Good Thai women, regardless of their chosen field or work, are helpful and more old-fashioned than their Western counterparts. They are more likely to see certain things — cooking, cleaning, laundry — as women's work. While many are also fashion-conscious, they do not make a spectacle of how they decorate their bodies. I would be very leery of women with tattoos, lots of gold jewelry, a nose job and showy clothes. (By the way, a Thai nose job is done to make the nose *bigger*.)

There are also some pretty obvious signs displayed by women (and men too, of course) who are troubled and should be avoided. Knife or razor scars on the arms and heavy drinking, gambling or drug use are obvious warnings.

"Nice" Thai women are quiet and shy around new people. They are religious, they don't smoke cigarettes or drink whiskey, they don't disappear daily for hours on end with vague excuses about where they have been, they are not exhibitionistic, they are not pushy about money (or anything, for that matter). They are respectful toward older people.

One extremely important thing to be careful about if you have met someone in a bar is "another man." Many bar girls have boy-friends, or even husbands, already. Sometimes they are Thai men, sometimes they are farangs. At the very least, this is a recipe for a broken heart. It could also be a recipe for some broken bones. Aside from becoming a paranoid spy, the only way to deal with this issue is to take your time. Remember that bar girls are working for money, and that fact does not preclude her having a man in her life already. Merely asking if she has someone already will not do the trick. She will tell you what you *want* to hear. If you are in Thailand on a holiday, it probably doesn't matter if she is attached — although you should certainly be careful. If you are looking for a serious relationship, that is another matter.

One of these individuals is a katoy... and one isn't. Which is which?

Surely you know that all who seem to be Thai women are not women at all. There are a lot of katoys in Thailand. A katoy is a transvestite, or perhaps a full-blown transsexual, or possibly something in transition. I am absolutely open-minded about who or what people sleep with. If you want a katoy, that is fine by me. If you want a woman, make sure it is a woman. Be warned, that even if you want a katoy, they are very often dangerous. A few weeks before this chapter was written, a German man was murdered by two katoys in his Bangkok hotel room.

I checked into a budget hotel near one of the entertainment areas on Sukhumvit Road. I hadn't been to Bangkok for a spell, and was looking forward to kicking up my heels. I put my suitcase in the room and immediately, without showering or anything, went around the corner for a beer in one of my favorite spots. A woman who worked the bar and who I had known for some time, spotted me and said hello. Then she asked me where I was staying. I told her. She said "Oh my God, what room?"

"Room 7," I replied, "why?"

"Oh no. Room 7? Really?"

"Yes. What's the matter?"

"Man die in that room three days ago. He go with two katoys and they kill him in the room. Very bad luck you stay there."

Well, I didn't know about luck, but the idea of a dude dying in the very room I was in — and only three days before — gave me a case of the willies. I immediately went back to the hotel and told them I didn't want to stay there. Since I had paid nothing and not used any of the facilities, they let me off the hook.

Several days later, I read in the paper that the police were still investigating the case of the German tourist who had been murdered by two katoys whom he had taken to his room.

Most Thai people love Thailand, as well they should. The idea of a Thai woman relocating to the West is something that should be thought about long and hard. I've heard tell of many a Thai woman who moved to America, Australia or elsewhere, and one of two things resulted — they turned into Western-type women in their approach to life or they beat feet back to Thailand in a real hurry. In addition to everything else, it is very difficult to make the necessary legal and political arrangements to take a Thai lady to many Western countries. This is particularly true of America, Australia and England.

I've found that it is best to be totally honest with Thai women. For example, if you are taking a lady for the night, tell her how much you are willing to pay, what you expect and how long you want her to stay with you. "I can only give you 500 baht, I want you to do X,Y and Z for me. And I do not want you to leave too early in the morning." Very few Thais will go back on a verbal agreement they have made.

Or, with a long-term girlfriend: "I can give you some money every month — maybe 2,000 baht, but no more. I can take care of you for a long time, but I cannot take care of your entire family."

I've already mentioned that there will most likely be a big education gap between you and your lady. There are three other huge gaps. One is age. Odds are that you are much older than your Thai sweetheart. Culture is another one. The West and the East approach things very differently. One's perception of time and what is considered polite are just two examples. Finally, there is language. Most problems between farangs and Thais are a matter of communication failure. It is very difficult to iron out misunderstandings if you only speak a bit of your partner's language.

I read a letter to the editor in the *Bangkok Post* from a Western woman bemoaning how "patriarchal" Thai society was, and how exploited Thai women were. I doubt seriously whether this woman lived in Thailand, and if she did, she paid little attention to what was happening around her. Thailand is different than the West, and Western categories are not appropriate here. Women have a great deal of power and influence in this country. They are, for example, represented in business and banking to a much greater extent than in the West. In the home as well, the Thai woman is valued and respected. The women of the Royal Family are highly regarded by all, and rightfully so. A very good case could be made that Thai women run the country — top to bottom. If Thailand is anything, it's a matriarchy.

Chapter Eight
Thai Men

By and large, Thai men walk softly but carry a big stick. They are usually handsome, thin but muscled, and have thick, black hair. They are often very athletic, and, even when older, can climb coconut trees unaided.

I have a great deal of respect for Thai men in general, but my knowledge of them is very limited. That is true of most ex-pats. The bottom line, I suspect, is that the lack of knowledge and communication is based on fear. Unfortunately, fear is a very negative emotion, and in the case of many ex-pats' attitudes toward, and dealings with, Thai men it results in prejudice and even hatred. I suggest that you try to avoid this.

When I first moved to Thailand, and even before, I thought it would be a good idea to make friends with some Thai men. The only Thais I knew to any extent were women, and that seemed like a situation that needed fixing. I tried to get to know some Thai fellows, and, to some extent succeeded. There were two guys in Phuket whom I was somewhat friendly with, and we occasionally did things together. Here in the bush, I have one man whom I would consider a friend. At the end of the day, though, the friendships are somewhat superficial. I think this is due to language and cultural differences. But, in addition to that, Thai men are just very different than Western men. It's hard to put one's finger on the difference. It is a kind of feeling of discomfort and uncertainty. Some ex-pats take this feeling so far that they actively dislike all Thai men, and it is not uncommon at all for an ex-pat bar owner to essentially ban Thai men from his establishment. I think that is very wrong.

Of course, making friends anywhere is not easy, and the older we get, the more that seems to be the case. But I remember reading somewhere about a man who had lived in Thailand for over six years. He liked it very much, but when it came time for him to leave, he realized that he had not made a single friend. For the male ex-pat, the situation is exacerbated relative to Thai men.

I have a number of Thai friends, but all except a few are women. Some of my friends are English students, others work in bars, one works in a travel agency, some are the wives of farang friends. The best Thai male friend I have is a bartender, and, as it turns out, he is gay. Even he is not someone I hang out with so much as he is someone whom I trust. He looked after my house when I was away, helped with cooking at birthday parties, and things like that. The problem with making friends with Thai men is that we have very little to talk about. We can talk a little about international sports, women and drinking. After that, there isn't much to say. We can't talk about politics or American football or the latest book we read or movie we saw. If you are interested in handyman things or motorbikes and such, that opens up some topics for conversation. Since I'm not particularly interested in conversations like that, there is very little left to say.

Living in rural Thailand as I do now has provided the opportunity to get to know some Thai men. Most of the ones I have dealings with are older (roughly my age). I have found that my interest in boxing (conventional, as well as muay Thai) is a common theme and ice breaker. The more I learn of the Thai language, the easier it is to make friends with Thai guys.

Finally, until you get to know someone fairly well, my advice concerning Thai men is to be nice, polite and smile and see if you have something in common. I don't think it is wise to get involved in heavy drinking sessions with Thai guys (or ex-pats, for that matter), or to constantly be the provider of cigarettes and beer. I don't think it is wise to be rude and macho with them. I don't think it is wise to have problems with them. As a foreigner, you absolutely cannot win if you have a problem with a Thai man — especially if it is a physical problem. I don't care if you have a black belt in karate and a body like Hercules, my advice in regard to fighting Thai guys is avoid it regardless of the cost to your ego. Among other things, Thai guys "cheat" in physical confrontations. They gang up on you, and don't hesitate to use bricks and boards and the like. They have a fairly long fuse, but when they get angry, it's in spades. They also have a long memory. If you really piss them off, they may wait months to get even. When they do, it may be something like vandalizing your motorbike, or, far worse, breaking your legs — with the help of several friends. Avoid problems with Thai men. Period.

Aside from that, you're on your own.

There was a German fellow in my bar in Phuket one night. He was quite drunk. Big and loud and wearing thick eyeglasses, he spoke excellent foul-mouthed Thai, and he liked to show it off. He began talking to some of the Thai ladies in my bar. I wasn't sure what he was saying because I have made it a point to *not* learn foul-mouthed Thai. It can only cause trouble.

It so happened that the very same night the German was in the bar, one of my Thai men friends was there too. He'd brought along three of his Thai friends. Dek was his name, and he was big and young and muscled, and word had it that he used to be a Thai boxer. Dek had rung the round-of-drinks-for-everybody bell a couple of times, and the Thai guys were simply having a good time. The German man went on and on, talking his foul-mouthed Thai to the ladies. Dek came up to me and said, "Is he a friend of yours?"

"No," I replied honestly, "I've never seen him before tonight."

Dek approached the German and confronted him about his rudeness to Thai women. He confronted him in an aggressive way. The German was intimidated, and was trying to defend himself verbally. He said he was only joking. Dek said he didn't think it was funny. The German didn't see the small Thai man who came up behind him and hit him over the head with a bottle, or the two other Thai men who began punching him.

They didn't beat the German up too badly. I've seen much worse. Maybe the guy got the message, though. Maybe not. He never came in my bar again, however, and that was just fine by me.

I'll say it again. You can't win in a fight with a Thai man. Even if you win, you lose — in the long run.

Chapter Nine
You Will Always
Be a Farang

"The Buddha said: 'Monk, you and you alone are your refuge. You and you alone are your pathway.'"[1]

Buddhism teaches that all of us ultimately walk alone. We must save ourselves. Unlike Christianity, which all farangs have incorporated into their thinking, no matter how religious or irreligious they may be, there is no redemption by someone else.

No matter where you go or what you do, the most frequently used Thai word you will hear is "farang."

The translation many dictionaries give for the Thai word "farang" is "foreigner." That is a bit misleading. The word comes from "farang set" which means "French." There are other, better words for "foreigner," but you rarely hear them.

Some people get a bee in their bonnet about being called a farang, and write lengthy tracts to the *Bangkok Post* complaining about the term. While it occasionally bothers me, mostly it doesn't, and I use the word frequently myself. It's a handy word, after all.

However, the word "farang" carries with it a lot of baggage that a dictionary can't tell you about. That is one of the reasons why some people get irritated about it. But it won't do you any good to get irritated and it is highly unlikely that you are going to "rehabilitate"

---

1 *The Monastic Life: Pathway of the Buddhist Monk*, Gerald Roscoe. Bangkok. Asia Books. p. 66.

the Thai language. Still, it is important to talk a little about what is in the suitcase labeled "farang."

For a long time, a situation of double-pricing existed in Thailand on both an institutional as well as an informal level. This meant that farangs were charged more than Asian people. And, let's make it very clear that the word farang does not include Malaysians, Indians, Japanese, Chinese or any other Asian group — thus, another reason why the word should not be translated as foreigner. One somewhat unusual example of institutional double-pricing can be found at banks. As of late 1995, certificates of deposit earned 10.5%... *if* you were a Thai! For foreigners, the rate was 9%! Interest rates in Thailand are generally higher than in the States.

Double-pricing means that farangs pay more than their Asian counterparts for goods or services. Institutional double-pricing (temples, parks, etc.) is gradually disappearing. This is due, in a large part, to an outcry from the farang community. Still, you read letters to the editor of the *Bangkok Post* complaining about how this or that attraction charges farangs more. Some Thai people will try to justify double-pricing by saying that farangs have more money. As a generalization, that may be true. Individually, it most certainly is not. Judging by the number of Mercedes and BMWs cruising the highways or gridlocked in Bangkok traffic, there are hundreds of thousands of Thais who have more money than I do. But the "justification" reflects an attitude that says all farangs are loaded with dough.

While institutional double-pricing is disappearing, it is alive and well in the private sector. From bars which have farang prices and Thai prices, to tuk-tuks which try to get 100 baht from a farang while a Thai will pay 20, it is something you will encounter every day. In shops and even hotels, the practice of double-pricing is widespread. What can you do about it? Here are a few suggestions.

First, like nearly everything in Thailand, it is almost always futile to get angry. If you "yak-yak" too much, it may even get you into trouble. Try nicely to negotiate a cheaper price. Until you get an idea about how much things cost, it is wise to make a habit of bargaining. As a rule of thumb, try offering half of the asking price.

Tuk-tuk drivers expect you to haggle the price.

Second, learn to speak some Thai that is related to asking how much things are. If you learn to say to a tuk-tuk driver, "How much to go to Patpong?" he will assume you've been in Thailand awhile, and is more likely to offer you a reasonable price.

Third, get a feel for how much things cost. Ask, listen and remember. At the restaurant, when the Thai man paid for his beer while you were drinking yours, how much did he pay? If you are charged more, the most you can do about it is ask why you are being charged more. Do it with a smile on your face. Personally, I generally don't even do that. I pay the inflated price and never go back to the restaurant.

Fourth, if you have a Thai friend, have that person help you in learning prices and negotiating bargains. If you have a Thai lady friend, she may be reluctant to do this at first. Gradually, as she sees that you are paying too much for things, she should help you. If she doesn't, you should wonder whether she has your best interests at heart.

When I lived in the States I did my best to combat racism and sexism. I think both states of mind are foul. But sometimes I struggled with trying to define these terms. *The Oxford Dictionary of Current English* says racism is the "belief in the superiority of a particular race; prejudice based on this" or "antagonism towards other races." The problem here lies with when and whether *pride* is an issue. Thais are a proud people. They're proud of their history and culture and independence from foreign domination — as well they should be. Does pride in what you are and where you come from make a person a racist? I don't think so. However, it is quite clear that farangs are different than Thais. That difference means that farangs are easily identified, and that their different approach to life is something that can be talked about.

Many farangs of the cynical type discussed in an earlier chapter believe that the Thai approach to life is inferior and that it is their mission in life to teach Thais the "correct" way to do things. The problem is that such farangs approach their "mission" in a way that is absolutely unacceptable by Thai standards. Direct and blatant criticism do not work here. Anger does not work. Claiming that the American, Australian or English way of doing things is superior to the Thai way does not work. Furthermore, it probably *isn't* superior — *in Thailand*. The cynical, and perhaps racist, ex-pat doesn't know that. But when his approach doesn't work and he makes a big scene, the most common reaction from a Thai is to explain his behavior on the grounds that he is a farang — even though many (hopefully most) farangs don't act like he does. So a kind of cycle of racism is initiated. The cynical and ignorant farang thinks Thais are stupid, and the Thai thinks farangs are crazy.

Suppose someone is building a house for you. You take my advice, and are at the construction site every day to make sure things are done well. The worker is laying bricks for the wall, and you're convinced that the way he is doing it is incorrect. How should you handle this?

The best way, to be honest, is to tell your Thai wife that you are not happy, and ask her talk to the man. She'll know how to do it the Thai way. Remember that it may be difficult for her to do this. She is probably younger than the worker, and she is a female. If, for whatever reason, it is not possible for her to help, you can try something like this:

Say to the worker, "I see that you are laying bricks now."

"Yes, I am."

"Do you think that the wall will be straight and strong?"

"Yes, I think it will be."

"I've never seen anyone lay bricks like that."

"That's the way I do it."

"Because I've never seen anyone lay bricks like that, I am a little worried. Can you help me?"

"What do you want me to do?"

Then, proceed to show him how you want the bricks laid. After you've shown him, ask him if he likes your way of doing things. When he says yes, which he will, thank him for helping you out.

Always try to make it seem as if *you* have the problem — not the worker. That's true in nearly every instance, including personal relationships. Ultimately, of course, when such situations arise, it *is* your problem.

One farang I know built a house in Phuket. He spent very little time supervising construction. He was too busy drinking or dashing off to Bangkok. Upon his return from one trip to Bangkok, he went to see how things were going with the house. He was totally dissatisfied with the way the windows had been installed. He took a sledge hammer and destroyed them. *That* is not the way to make your point anywhere in the world — never mind Thailand.

As with any couple, my wife and I have had some problems and disagreements. On occasions it has been something to do with her family — two times, it had to do with her mother. This is sacred territory for Thais. On both occasions, I made it clear in a Thai way that I was unhappy about something. I did this simply by being quieter than usual, not smiling as much and leaving the house for hours at a time. In America, this approach would be frowned on — especially by psychological types and counseling freaks. In Thailand, it works. Eventually, my wife asked me what was the matter. After several, "Oh, nothing's," I told her that I had a problem. I told her that I knew this was Thailand, and that I must do things the Thai way, but sometimes that made me unhappy. I didn't know what to do. After the usual "It's up to you's," things moved on. I said, "No, it isn't up to me. It's your family, it's Thailand. It is my problem, not yours."

Within no time, my wife had a talk with her mother, the issue was resolved and I no longer had a problem. Thais can be great compromisers and problem solvers if you give them a chance. Things do usually work out, especially if you don't approach them with the quick-fix Western attitude.

I knew a man in Pattaya who had a similar problem arise concerning his mother-in-law. He kept it inside himself for days, and then one day, with the mother-in-law present, he exploded and told his wife off, slammed his fists into doors and cursed the mother-in-law. His wife left him and went to work in the bars. The farang approach to things recommended by social-science types, women's magazines, relationship counselors and the like, wouldn't work either. It's Thailand. Do it the Thai way.

One reason the word "farang" can be sometimes irritating is because we hear it so often. Everywhere we go we can hear the word or read it on people's lips. Couple that with the fact that most of the time we don't know what is being said about the farang, and we have a breeding ground for paranoia.

Imagine for a moment that you are bald and that the Thai words for bald guy are the same as the English words. (They aren't, of course.) Suppose you are having a meal in a restaurant, and overhear a conversation among four Thai people. In the space of 20 minutes, you hear the words "bald guy" 28 times. Sometimes it's accompanied with laughter. You understand none of the conversation but the phrase "bald guy." Are you going to wonder what's going on? No doubt. Are you going to have pangs of paranoia? Probably.

Most farangs want to be individuals. Sometimes when someone calls me a farang, I want to say, "I am not a farang, I am Michael." No one wants to be categorized, but categorizing people and things is part of human nature. Keep your cool and keep smiling and it will all go away.

When all is said and done, there is really nothing you can do about being a farang. Most of the time, you won't mind. You'll use the word yourself, as I have in this book. You'll have your ups and downs about everything in Thailand — just as you would in Chicago, London or Perth. Finally, it's just as easy for you to categorize Thai people and Thailand as it is for them to categorize you. Try to keep your negative feelings to yourself. Try to think of things as being your problem. Try to avoid hostility and confrontation.

Farangs who make an effort to learn Thai customs and etiquette are nearly always treated well. Whether you like it or not, as a farang you represent all other farangs in the country. It is difficult enough to adjust and learn and make friends without having to follow a farang who has created problems with Thais. Please be polite, don't lose your temper, and smile a lot — no matter how certain you are that you've been done wrong.

Going Home

The first time that you will become acutely aware that you are a person without a country is the first time you return to your native land. For most ex-pats, it is an odd or even surreal experience. The longer it has been since you've been home, the stranger it will seem.

The most striking thing about going home will probably be when you realize that no one — family, friends or strangers — understands what you are up to and what Thailand is all about. At best, you'll get a superficial understanding. At worst, you'll get blank-eyed disinterest. Thailand is so very different than Western countries, few people have the necessary handles for understanding it.

When you realize that Thomas Wolfe was right when he said, "You can't go home again," you have just become a certified ex-pat. Once an ex-pat, always an ex-pat is something that all of us know.

Whenever I leave the small village that I call home to venture to Udon, Bangkok or even farther afield, I must first take the bus from the small city of Ban Dung. Of course I return by bus as well.

When I return to Ban Dung by bus, I am usually pretty conspicuous as the only farang passenger. Generally, I am greeted by a handful, sometimes a mob, of samlor drivers anxious to give me a ride to my village. They are also anxious to make more money than they normally do, because it is standard procedure to charge farangs more.

Samlors galore await... don't let them overcharge you!

I know that a samlor to the village that I live in should cost 30 baht — 40 at the most. The first few times I arrived in Ban Dung, I tried to bite the bullet, negotiate a fair price and be on my way. Sometimes I was successful, sometimes not. It was always an irritating and tension-producing situation, however.

Now, when I arrive in Ban Dung, I take my bag and get off the bus. I smile and say hello to the samlor drivers in Thai, but walk over to a nearby food stall, sit down and order a coffee or cold drink and wait. That alone usually reduces the number of drivers pursuing me to two or three. At that point, something naturally develops — for example, a driver asks where I live (in Thai). I respond in Thai, and perhaps we get into a brief conversation. Within five or ten minutes, using this natural, easygoing approach, I invariably have a ride home at a fair price. I have also drastically reduced the hassle factor.

Take your time. Be reasonable. Sit down for a minute and see what happens. It's a lot easier on the blood pressure.

Sometimes, especially in rural Thailand, it is fun to be different. To be the farang. To get the wide-eyed stares and read people's lips when they say "farang." Sometimes it is difficult. You'd just like to blend in. Only occasionally is it annoying. I believe, however, that farangs are accepted in Thailand far better than Thais, and other non-white people, are accepted in the U.S. Now that I live in Thailand, I am more proud than ever to be an American. I'm not proud of American politicians and the like. But the American people are, by and large, a good lot. There are some, however, who are racist and xenophobic. I think my wife would encounter many more difficulties living in America than I have in Thailand. I am absolutely amazed at how well I have been received in this tiny, rural Thai village. Here, I am Michael first and a farang second. I like that.

Chapter Ten
Buddhism

Thai culture and society are woven into a fabric that is rich, colorful and diverse. The framework — the loom — that it is woven on is Buddhism.

It is impossible to live in Thailand without coming into constant contact with Buddhism. Over 90% of the population are Buddhist.[1] The majority practice Theravada Buddhism — the older school.

Everywhere you go there are temples, monks, Buddha images and images of revered figures from the history of Thailand and Buddhism. For the open-minded, and those interested in learning, there is no better place than Thailand to study this tolerant and helpful philosophy.

Thais are very spiritual people. They are also very understanding of other forms of religion and the world of the unseen. They are reluctant to dismiss approaches to the universe that predate Buddhism, and consequently there is a rich fabric of belief and metaphysics all woven together. Some of this, Hindu elements and animism for example, aren't, strictly speaking, Buddhism.

The founder of Buddhism was Siddhartha Gautauma. He was born in Northern India, now part of Nepal, more than 2,500 years ago.

---

1 There is no discrimination against the minority Muslims or Christians or other groups in Thailand.

Hinduism was the dominant religion of India at the time, and Buddhism still has much in common with it. After going on a spiritual search for the cause of human suffering, Siddhartha became enlightened. The word "buddha" means "enlightened one." Consequently, you will hear people referring to many figures as Buddha. There are buddhas taken from Hinduism, from Chinese philosophy and from Thai history. The "fat buddha," for example, is Phra Song Ga Jai, from China. You will also see figures of the fifth king of Thailand. Thais call him Law Ha, and he was a wonderful man whom everyone should revere.

It is up to you whom you decide to show *special* devotion to. Which figures you have in your home or shop and offer flowers and incense to is a matter of choice. There are no competitions or arguments about which buddha is better. All buddhas are honored.

Buddha images are not idols. They should be treated with respect at all times. Before touching or cleaning one, a person should wait. Never place a buddha on the floor, hang or drape things on them (other than flowers), or climb on big ones.

Buddhism teaches that good actions bring good results, and bad actions bring bad results. This is, of course, the law of karma, and it carries on from one lifetime to the next. Buddha laid down some suggestions as to how to try to be a good person and thus minimize suffering, and all good Buddhists should *try* to follow those suggestions. The emphasis is on the word "try." Since Buddhists, like Christians, are human beings, they usually fail. This doesn't make them sinners, as with popular Christianity. The precepts that Buddha laid down are something that people should make an effort to live up to. How hard they try is up to them. Even the Buddha himself allowed that his was only one path of many.

Farangs are welcome to participate in Buddhist ceremonies, enter the temple and even become monks. There is no prejudice against outsiders involving themselves in Buddhist activity. If you aren't sure what to do or how to behave in a given situation, simply watch what the Thais do. Even if you make a mistake, normally there is no problem, because Thais understand that you are a farang and appreciate your sincere efforts.

Novice monk in a temple in Phrae.

There are two kinds of reactions from farangs to Buddhism which I think are not fruitful, and are perhaps even negative. The first one, and the worst, is to dismiss Buddhism in all its forms, refuse to participate at all and condemn it out of hand as foolish and superstitious. At the very least, the farang who reacts this way fails to learn something about the very epicenter of Thai culture. At the worst, he seriously offends Thai people. Thais are not demanding, and neither is Buddhism. There is no effort to convert people to Buddhism, and Thais are more than willing to let you approach life your own way, as long as you make an effort to be moral. If you are an agnostic or even an atheist, you should not let this stop you from involving yourself in Buddhism. Buddha himself said that he was not God, and Thais don't hold that he is. He was enlightened, and because of his good heart and special deeds he is to be remembered and revered.

The second negative reaction to Buddhism — something that may seem positive — is to make a show out of it. Many farangs end up wearing huge golden "buddha necklaces," and getting tattoos of various buddhas. (Law Ha is popular with farangs.) I suppose if a person is serious about honoring buddhas in this way, there is nothing wrong with it. Most Thais who I know, however, think it rather odd that a beer-drinking, womanizing farang who rarely sets foot in a temple adorns himself with buddhas. Before you go roaming about making a spectacle of yourself, it is probably better to know what you are doing. In fact, it is generally better *never* to make a show or spectacle of anything, just as it is best never to brag. Modesty, the middle path of Buddhism, is best in Thailand — probably everywhere, for that matter.

I would like to add that I believe it is critical to have a strong spiritual element in our lives — to recognize that there are things beyond our control and knowledge. Even though I have a Christian background, I value and appreciate the role of Buddhism. I have no problem participating in Buddhist ceremonies and having Buddha images in my home. There is no contradiction there, as far as I'm concerned. These things add meaning and substance to my life. I don't think any particular religion has a monopoly on "the truth," but

I do believe that faith and loving kindness contribute immensely to our lives. I know that without a spiritual perspective, it would have been impossible for me to undertake this adventure. So, with all due respect to my atheist friends, I encourage you to investigate the Buddhist perspective. There's nothing to lose by looking.

Thailand is a hierarchical society. At the top of the hierarchy are monks. They are easily recognized in their saffron or brown robes and their shaved heads. Monks are to be treated with respect at all times. Women are never to touch monks. Even when handing them something, it should not be done directly, but the item should be set down so the monk can pick it up.

In Thailand, women are not allowed to become monks. Those who want to lead a monastic life, can opt to become nuns. Nuns generally wear white robes and their hair is very close-cropped like that of a monk. While nuns are not part of the Sangha, or community of monks, they should be treated respectfully.

As to whether there is sexism in refusing ordination to woman, I prefer to leave the issue up to good, practicing Buddhists. Fault-finders and intellectual imperialists bent on reforming the world in their image can prattle on all they want to about the issue. The Thais will do things their own way and in their own time. This is as it should be.

Nearly all Thai males become monks for at least one period in their lives. It may be as short a time as a few weeks, or it may be for a lifetime. Neither monks nor nuns take a lifetime vow. Many people become monks or nuns several times during their lives.

There are farang monks in Thailand, but it is unusual to see one. Several temples in Thailand "specialize" in helping farangs become monks and/or learn meditation. Among them are Wat Mahathat in Bangkok, Wat Ram Poeng in Chiang Mai, Wat Nong Pa Pong in Ubon Ratchathani and Wat Suan Mok near Surat Thani.

Spirit Houses

Part of the fabric that constitutes Thai spirituality involves beliefs that probably predate Buddha. Plainly put, most Thais believe in spirits or, if you like, ghosts. There are many different kinds of ghosts — good ones, bad ones, spirits of deceased people and so forth. Thais take these beliefs quite seriously. The most visible manifestations of Thai belief in spirits are "spirit houses."

Homemade spirit house.

Sometimes lovely and ornate, other times simple and homemade, the buildings themselves are typically done in Thai-style architecture. Most are about the size of a doll house. Many of the houses are white with colorful trim. Others are red or brown.

Regardless of their construction or size, they are special buildings for special beings. You see, Thailand is a place that is inhabited not only by people, animals and plants, but by other beings as well. There are many different kinds of these other beings, but they all share one characteristic — they are not normally visible to people. One sort of being Thais call "phee," which we might translate as "ghost." There are also "phra poom." Translating "phra poom," like translating nearly any phrase, is difficult, if not impossible. Perhaps the best translation is "spirit of the land." Part of the significance of the Thai phrase can be understood by the word "phra" — a word used for important, respected and good figures in Thailand. Thus we have Phra Phoot Tha Jao (Lord Buddha), Phra Yeh Soo (Jesus), Phra Jao Yo Hua (King) and so forth. So phra poom are special, and good, beings or spirits.

Phra poom, as well as phee, are not really Buddhist concepts. While the vast majority of Thais are Buddhists, spirit houses and a belief in ghosts are not part of the teachings of Buddha. Many people theorize that a belief in phra poom and other spirits dates back more than two millennia to a time before Buddha's teaching came to Thailand — a time when most of the inhabitants practiced different forms of animism. But Thais are extremely open-minded, and sometimes eclectic in the expression of their religious views, so most see no problem or contradiction in being Buddhists and believing in phra poom as well.

Every piece of land in Thailand is occupied by phra poom, in addition to other spirits. When and if people decide to occupy that land and build a house or other structure, it is a good idea for them to pay their respects to the phra poom which are already there or which they would like to have come and stay. This can be done simply by lighting incense and kneeling in respect at a special place on the land, or it can be done by setting up a sahn phra poom or "spirit house."

Most spirit houses stand on a pedestal, and while there is no set formula, they usually have furniture, perhaps a few servants, and elephants or water buffalo. Maybe dancing ladies for entertainment would be nice. Like any house, the spirit house requires various things which we should lovingly give to the phra poom. What it needs is partly the result of the personalities of the phra poom who live there. Flowers are usually appreciated, and so is food, so long as it is vegetarian. Water or soft drinks may also be offered.

Thai people tend to have a somewhat fatalistic — or accepting — approach to life. They do not complain, whine and cry as much as people in the West. There is very little psychologizing, and I expect that opening a counseling practice in Thailand would probably not be lucrative. Thais are, by and large, emotionally self-sufficient. That does not mean that they don't have personal problems. It does mean, however, that they have an approach to life which is extremely useful in dealing with, if not solving, those problems. That approach is Buddhism. It is faith. Don't miss out on the opportunity to incorporate some of that faith into your own life.

Ancient ruins of Sukothai.

Chapter Eleven
Time and Everyday Life

Time is a relative notion. Fortunately, the inflexible Western interpretation of time is not the only one in the universe. Encompassing all concepts of time is *cosmic* time. Thai standard time comes closer to cosmic time than farang standard time.

If you have spent any time at all in Thailand, you are well aware that Thai people do not perceive time in the same way as farangs do. Of course, this means that they have not been regimented into tightly-constructed schedules. It also means a number of other things — not the least of which is the fact that Thais are often "late" by farang standards, and think absolutely nothing of having to wait for things or people. Waiting is a way of life in Thailand. I suspect that Thais don't object because it gives them a chance to take a break, talk with friends or simply watch the world go by. One of the most appealing things about Thailand is the casual attitude toward time. It also happens to be one of the most frustrating things. If you want things to be done by the clock, Thailand is not the place for you to live. If you expect people to always be on time for engagements, you are in for a rude awakening. There is a price to be paid for the easygoing and laid-back lifestyle of Thailand. I do not intend for this to be a negative chapter, and I am more than willing to make the trade-off in order to be less stressed-out and agitated in general. Still, there are situations, usually small ones but always daily, that you will encounter during your adventure in Thailand. Knowing about these scenarios and then accepting them will help you. One thing is certain: You won't change them.

As in most tropical countries, the pace of life is much slower in Thailand. People walk and work slowly, and I have never seen anything vaguely resembling a hyperactive Thai person. The heat, of course, probably has a lot to do with this. Because nearly everything and everyone moves slowly, it is nearly impossible to get things done quickly — *anything* — so you may just as well forget that idea.

Depending on where you live, a typical day varies a great deal. One factor that does not vary is that everything happens slowly.

For those who live in a holiday destination, daily life is different than it is in rural Thailand. It most certainly is not typical of the way most Thai people live.

If you live in Patong Beach in Phuket, for example, perhaps your day will go something like this: You will wake up about 12 noon or 1 o'clock in the afternoon. You'll go out for "breakfast," but not be finished until 2 or 3 in the afternoon because the cook hasn't arrived at the restaurant yet and you'll have to wait for her. Unless you are at a beach resort like Phuket and enjoy swimming and sunbathing, now comes the most difficult part of the day — what to do in the daytime? It's no different in Bangkok, except you can substitute "shopping" for "swimming and sunbathing." So, next on your itinerary is killing a couple of hours. If you have to go to the bank or post office, that will help, because those simple little errands will probably take you at least an hour or two. Somewhere around 4 or 5, you'll have a quiet beer or two. They'll be quiet beers because nothing is really rolling at this time of day. Then, you'll probably take a little nap. After waking up and showering, you'll go out to eat. You won't get exactly what you want to eat, because the restaurant will be out of what you were really in the mood for.

About 9 or 10 at night, people begin to wake up. You'll start your evening at a bar — a friend's, or (if you've made a mistake and bought one yourself) your own bar. You'll drink, and then about midnight go for a walkabout and drink more. Your evening out will end about 3 or 4 AM, and you'll return home to sleep or participate in extracurricular activities. Occasionally, you will have a quiet night.

You'll either stay home or only go out briefly. You'll try to go to bed at midnight or so, but you'll be unable to sleep, so you'll read or watch a video. Even if you live and work in Phuket, Pattaya, etc., your daily schedule will be a variation on this theme, because that is the way these places are set up. It is nearly impossible to break this (vicious) cycle.

Daily life in the *real* Thailand is quite different. You'll wake up about 6 AM, make your own (instant) coffee and perhaps something to eat. What you do with your time during the day depends on many factors. I work in the garden, help my wife with her general store, go to the market and work on the computer. Most days I am busy doing something — although again, everything happens slowly. Because my wife is usually busy with the shop, I generally do some laundry and housework. I'll drink my beers in the late afternoon, eat dinner about 7 and go to bed about 10.

A number of things may have happened during the day. For starters, I may have been awakened at 4:30 or 5 AM by someone calling my wife's name because they wanted something from the shop. Thai people usually do not think *anything* about waking someone up — any time of day or night. Sometime in the course of the day, a pickup truck complete with a loudspeaker might drive around selling something — anything from watermelons to refrigerators. You may think that sort of thing happens only in bigger cities. It doesn't. Rural Thailand has its share of loudspeakers, music and wandering salesmen and -women. By and large, it is pretty quiet, but interruptions are common, and Thais usually think of them as interesting diversions. That's your best approach, too.

If I had to go to the bank that day, and it happened to be a Monday or the day after a long weekend, I would have been confronted by the following: Somewhere between ten and 50 people would be hanging around outside the bank and an equal number inside. Once in the bank, I'd see no semblance of a line, but a lot of people would be sitting or standing and waiting. I planned ahead enough to bring my own pen, so I wouldn't have to wait for one while a Thai person *very* slowly filled out their deposit or withdrawal form. I would have filled out my form, inched my way up to a teller and left it on the counter, making sure to catch his eye. Rather than wait for the transaction to be completed, like most of the other people in the bank were doing, I'd go off to do errands. On a slow day at the bank, the transaction would be completed in five minutes or so. On a busy day, it could take more than an hour. Stacks of money are thrown into and taken out of drawers, assorted supervisors sign forms and, plainly put, utter chaos reigns. If one of my errands was to go to the post office, I might well have been confronted with a similar situation there. I would return to the bank and hopefully they would have finished with the transaction. I catch the teller's eye again and would get my bank book back. You may as well get used to all of this, because it is the norm, and no change is in sight. The key is to adapt, plan ahead and try to keep smiling.

Now, you may be saying to yourself that Thais do everything slowly except their driving. I'll grant you that many Thais drive fast, but I think my point still holds true if you are talking about getting someplace. That very often happens slowly. Traffic jams, push-carts holding things up, road construction, slow trucks, parades and more mean that frequently you will get where you are going at a snail's pace. By my lights, one reason to have a motorbike instead of a car is that you can more easily avoid obstacles.

Thais divide the twenty-four-hour day into four six-hour segments, although two twelve-hour segments are becoming more common. For example, 8 PM is 2 o'clock in the evening, because one of the four segments of time begins at 6 PM. Instead of having noon and midnight, after both of which it becomes one o'clock, there is morning (6 AM), afternoon (12 noon), evening (6 PM), and night (midnight), after each of which it becomes one o'clock (in the evening, morning, etc.). Obviously, this can lead to confusion. If an appointment is important to you, make certain that the time is fully understood. But don't let the fact that Thais have four time compartments for the day delude you into thinking that they compartmentalize their lives the way farangs do. Everyone in the world eats, sleeps, works and plays. Farangs put these activities into boxes. Thais don't. They may sleep at work, or eat or play. If they're hungry and at work, they'll eat — usually with a group of other workers. And yes, it does seem to me that Thais eat a lot and do so without gaining weight. They also work long hours, making every effort to have fun while doing so. In fact, the word for work and the word for party is the same in Thai — *ngan*. And Thais love to party as well. This refreshing approach to time colors every aspect of Thai life. Want to drink whiskey at seven in the morning? No problem. Leave work to go see a sick friend? Go ahead. Spontaneity is the key to Thais' perception of time. No people on earth are more spontaneous. You're not going to change that about Thai people either, and even if you could, I'd ask you not to.

Young childhood is a time in the life of Thai people when everything is taken care of for them. Plainly put, young children in Thailand are, by Western perspectives, spoiled. Not in a bratty, American kind of way, but in the sense that young children get all the attention, affection and sympathy that they want. That's good, because later in life, Thais work hard and expect very little in return. By the age of eight or nine, Thai children are carrying their own weight around the home — especially girls. By the age of 14, they are working very hard and often full-time. They don't kick up a fuss, and they don't moan. If they did, no one would listen. Neither do they boast. That's bad news too.

There is another stage in the Thai life cycle, and that is old age — beginning about 60. Elderly people in Thailand are esteemed, listened to and helped. They know things the rest of us do not — things about this world as well as the world of the unseen.

Death, of course, does not end the cycle. It is just another part of it, because in death comes rebirth. If you have an opportunity to attend a Buddhist funeral, you should by all means do so. In the evening after the funeral, and for two days afterward, there is a party. The reason, of course, is to help cheer up the relatives. People eat, drink and play games. It can be an enjoyable time and the only suggestion that I can make, other than participating, is to not wear loud clothing.

Chapter Twelve
Toward A Philosophy
Of Money

Indeed, money can buy us neither love nor happiness. But think about it, we must. Particularly in Thailand.

Previous chapters dealt with costs and jobs. The purpose of this chapter is to write about money in both a philosophical and psychological way.

Thailand is semi-officially classified as a newly-industrialized country. That means that the infrastructure is good, but, for the most part, not up to the standards of the United States or England. Problems exist with communications and consumerism. It also means that Thailand is in a period of transition into a full-blown money economy.

Consumption

Mass communication has exposed nearly all Thais to consumer goods. Electronic items, the latest fashions, booze, cars, cigarettes and fancy homes are obviously all known to Thai people, and like people in the rest of the world, many Thais seek to own these things. Even in rural Thailand, where it is possible to live on next to nothing and not be ravaged by the kind of poverty found in big cities all over the world, Thais are aware of and long for motorbikes, TVs, refrigerators and assorted gizmos. All of these things are available in Thailand, but you should be aware that service, quality and honoring guarantees are all areas that, by and large, Thailand needs to improve greatly. Here are a few personal examples:

I bought a basic water pump for my well. Within two weeks after I bought it, it no longer functioned. I went to the shop where I had purchased it to seek help. The owner of the shop simply told me that there was no way he could have known it was faulty, and there was nothing he could do about it. So, what did I do? With the help of two friends, I made a new gasket from a motorbike inner tube and fixed it myself.

I bought a brand-new motorbike. After owning it for a month, I took it into the authorized dealer for service. They said they were sorry, but they couldn't service the bike that day because they had no motor oil. What did I do? I went to a place that had motor oil, and that is where I take my motorbike now for all of its servicing.

I bought a new bed complete with a mattress. Within two weeks the mattress sagged as though it were 30 years old. What did I do? I got used to sleeping on a lumpy mattress. I also, hopefully, learned for the one-hundredth, but last time, that in Thailand, more than in many places, you get what you pay for.

These experiences are not exceptions, they are the rule. Be extremely careful when you buy things. You will almost never get satisfaction from complaining or returning faulty merchandise. There are no consumer rights in Thailand, and it is essentially "too bad" if you are cheated, lied to, misled or misinformed. *Caveat emptor* is true in spades here.

The farangs that most Thais meet are here on holiday, and like most holiday-makers they have money to burn. Even farang ex-pats have more money than most Thais. Unless they have a work permit, farangs do very little in the way of work. When you combine Thailand's new philosophy of materialism with the experiences of Thai people with tourists or well-heeled foreigners, you have the potential for a problem of sorts. That problem is the fact that many Thais will see you as a walking, talking ATM machine. Some Thais (the occasional bar girl, for example) think that they have the ATM card *and* the key number to operate you. Hopefully, you won't be as foolish as one fellow I know who actually gave his Visa card to his girlfriend, along with the key number, and asked her to withdraw no more that 1,000 baht a day. I don't have to tell you about the debacle that resulted from this. It's quite predictable.

A more likely manifestation of farang-ATM syndrome is that you will frequently be asked for cigarettes or liquor, or that it will be assumed that it is you who is paying the tab at the restaurant. The restaurant bill is a little different, because it is customary in Thailand that the person with the most money pays the bill. Having people hit you up for smokes or beer or assorted other goodies is another matter. By and large, it is not something that Thais do to one another. It is strictly a result of the farang-ATM syndrome. There isn't a great deal you can do about this, but here are a few suggestions that might help in the long run:

Remember to always follow Buddha's middle path. Moderation is the key. If you act, especially initially, as if you are a moneybags, that is the way you will be treated for a very long time. Even if you are having a wild and crazy night on the town, if you set the wrong precedent it will be assumed that you are loaded with dough for life and that you can take care of everyone's family, friends and assorted hangers-on. This applies not just to the bar girl whom you've known for one evening, but to your fiancée's family when you make the first visit to her home. For heaven's sake, there is no reason for you to give Mama and Papa 50,000 baht, buy big brother a tuk-tuk and little sister a motorbike, and throw a big party for the entire village. If you do that, you are in for a lifetime of inflated expectations. Even if you want to live up to those expectations, I think it is bad news to issue a ticket on the gravy train for anyone — even people that you love. Besides all that, you are making life difficult for other farangs by setting a bad example and raising the cost of everything.

If you go to a bar or restaurant frequented by Thais (especially men) and leave your package of smokes on the bar or table, odds are good that people will just help themselves. If you find this annoying — and I certainly do — the solution is as simple as putting them in your pocket. Sure, some people will ask for one. In that case you can do several things. Give them one, tell them no, ask them why they don't buy their own (with a smile on your face, of course) or ignore

them by smiling and talking to someone else. This section about
cigarettes may seem trivial, and I suppose it is. Daily doses of
occurrences such as this, however, can become tiresome. In addition,
it symbolizes a perception that I am trying to inform you about.

Unless you give every Thai everything that you are asked for, it is
inevitable that you will be called a "Cheap Charlie." The Thai word is
"kee neow." Literally, that means "sticky shit" in Thai. Odds are
pretty good that anyone who calls you kee neow to your face is a rude
money grubber, and you shouldn't give it a second thought. There are
a number of retorts you can make to such a person, but I wouldn't
bother. Remember, polite, nice Thai people do not aggressively
criticize people to their faces. Just because they aren't being nice and
polite doesn't mean you shouldn't be.

There is another side to this issue that should be mentioned. By
and large, Thais are extremely generous and communal in their
approach to life. If they have something, they frequently share it with
others — whether it is booze, cigarettes, food, tools or their television
set, Thai people are apt to think of it as a community resource. It is
difficult for them to understand what they see as extreme
possessiveness in farangs. In spite of all the information about
cigarettes listed above, I have to confess to having bummed my share
of smokes from Thais. Thais have often shared their whiskey and
food with me. They have loaned me their motorbikes or tools. When I
built my house in Isaan, I used my neighbor's electricity until mine
was installed. Do not be a true Cheap Charlie. Be helpful and
generous in the same way that Thai people are. You know the
difference between being a tightwad and being a spendthrift. Apply
that to your daily life and you will have no problems.

A friend of mine named Ken, who was not loaded with money,
moved to a small village in Northern Thailand. It so happened that
there was another farang living with his Thai wife in the same village.
His name was Randy. Randy had a big two-story house with all the
amenities. Ken was building a simple, one-story dwelling. When
Randy had first moved to the village, he bought beers, whisky,
smokes and food for everyone who asked and for a lot who didn't. He
bought a pickup truck for his brother-in-law and a rice farm for his

father-in-law. After two years of give, give, giving, he was angry. He constantly complained that he could get no respect from his family or anyone in the village. Apparently he thought that respect was something a person could buy. His anger was exacerbated by the fact that Thais say "thank you" far less often than farangs do. Life was tough for Randy, and he frequently griped to Ken about his plight. Ken, on the other hand, had it difficult for the first several months he was in the village. No one said anything to his face, but he heard rumblings about him being a Cheap Charlie. He rarely bought drinks for anyone or offered cigarettes around. His widowed mother-in-law lived in a house with no electricity. Ken didn't like the rumblings, but he grew accustomed to them and slowly the Thai people in the village began to respect him. Several times, they even opened up and told him that they thought Randy was crazy for wasting so much money. Randy continued to blow money left and right. Eventually, his money ran low and he went to Bangkok to look for work. He spent more time in bars than he did circulating his resumé. Finally, the last of his money gone, he returned to Australia. His huge house is sitting in the village empty. No one can afford to buy it. Randy's wife returned to Bangkok to work in the bar where they'd met.

Should you ever move to the bush in Thailand, these are good things to remember: Keep things simple and, as always in Thailand, move slowly. If you move into a tiny neighborhood, build a huge house, buy a satellite dish and a new car, and throw money around, imagine what your neighbors will think. It is not a good idea to make a show of prosperity in Thailand. Granted, there are plenty of nouveau riche Thais who do make a show of things. It is not, however, wise for a farang to do so. Many Thais already have misconceptions about farangs and their money, and there is no need for you to verify those misconceptions. Again, modesty and the middle path are the key.

Chapter Thirteen
Fear, Paranoia, Anger and Procrastination

Fear is one of the most destructive of all emotions. Anger and guilt are two others.

What you have done or hope to do — move to Thailand — takes a lot of courage and energy. All real-life adventures do. Because it takes courage and energy, there is an emotional price to be paid for your decision. That price is probably higher than you imagined, and consequently it may result in some unproductive emotions and attitudes rearing their ugly heads.

Most people know that human beings have a fear of the unknown. In Thailand, there are many things that you don't understand or know, and therefore may become afraid of. There are institutional things such as police, bureaucrats and immigration officials. There are the phenomena of culture and language. A little anxiety never hurt anyone. It can be a motivating force and a challenge. You are, after all, starting a new life, and no one said that it would be easy. Unfortunately, there are some ex-pats who are driven by fear and turn into cowards. They become paralyzed by fear, and sometimes let others take a fall for them. The only way to combat fear and other negative emotions is to have a perspective to throw at them. A fact is something you can't do anything about. Your attitude, though, *is* under your control. As Karl Menninger said, "Attitudes are more important than facts."

In the first place, remember that you are a person with courage and energy. You've proven that by making a decision that very few people on earth have the guts to make. Secondly, many of the horror stories that you hear about ex-pats getting in trouble are either lies or the result of stupidity on the part of the ex-pat. If you are a person who has, by and large, stayed out of trouble in your life in your native land, you will probably have no trouble in Thailand. Finally, remember that all adventures contain monsters and dragons. When I encounter one, I try to remember what Nietzsche said: "Whatever doesn't kill me, makes me stronger." Stronger, in many cases, means gaining knowledge. The more you know, the less of the unknown there is to be afraid of.

Many ex-pats acquire a case of a disease that is a second cousin to fear. That disease is paranoia. I use the word "disease" because I want to emphasize that this is a feeling of uneasiness — of dis-ease. When I discussed the word "farang" in an earlier chapter, I mentioned how easy it was to be uncomfortable around Thai people who use the word "farang" a lot. In addition to that, there are other things that can bring on paranoia. As you know, Thais are not as directly confrontational as farangs are. That does not mean that they don't communicate anger. It simply means that they usually do it indirectly — personally, or through a third party. Because, beginning days after you arrive in Thailand, you will hear horror stories about what happened to other ex-pats, it is simple for you to have a mindset fertile for planting paranoia. You will hear stories of guys who had their penises cut off by jealous girlfriends, of people who were set up to be busted for drugs, of people being denied visas or deported, having their legs broken for not paying a debt and so forth. These kind of stories are common and, once in a blue moon, they may be true. The fact of the matter is this: Thailand is no more violent than anyplace else. It is *less* violent than many places. There are no more innocent people in Thai jails than there are in other countries. It is easier to get a Thai visa and live in Thailand than it is in most other countries. And so it goes. Again, as with the problem of fear, if you are a decent and polite human being, the odds are that you will get along fine. Thais are, on the whole, terrifically tolerant people, and most farangs who get into trouble in Thailand ask for it.

Aside from stupidity, the way the majority of farangs ask for problems is by getting angry. Direct and hostile confrontations are frowned on in Thailand. That doesn't mean they don't happen. It does mean that they are not cool. They are not cool because the issue of "face" comes into play. It is not at all wise to publicly and angrily criticize Thais or Thailand. Only three things can result from this: 1. By far, the most common result is that the Thais will leave and make every effort to have nothing to do with you because they consider you crazy; 2. They

A Bangkok police officer keeps the peace.

will feel trapped and have no choice but to get directly violent with you; and, 3. They will get even in a covert and subtle way.

Of course, there are many things in daily life which are frustrating and anger-producing. To remain sane and avoid reaching a boiling point, you will need some way to channel your anger. In an earlier chapter I wrote about indirect, Thai-style criticism. In addition to that, you need someone to bounce your anger (or fear, or paranoia) off of. The best and closest person is your sweetheart or spouse. If they are good and solid, they will help you. If they constantly say, "What can I do?" or "It's up to you," you might consider trading them in on a new model.

Because of the language barrier and cultural differences, however, ex-pat friends are also essential. They are the only ones on earth who truly know what you are going through. They occasionally get angry and discouraged just like you do.

Always remember that negative emotions tend to run in cycles. Sometimes (hopefully for only brief periods) you will be totally bummed-out on Thailand and your adventure. Most of the time (hopefully) you will feel like you are one of the luckiest people in the world. You live a good life in a wonderful country. If you are truly negative about your adventure, go home. If not, wait the cycle out and turn to people close to you for conversation in the meantime.

Procrastination can be a problem anywhere and everywhere. It just happens to be very easy to do in Thailand. There are several reasons for this. Weather is one of them. Tropical climates are not conducive to hyperactive, compulsive behavior. Thai people's easygoing and laid-back attitude is something that is very simply acquired. Thais do what needs doing, but they seldom seem pressured or rushed. Another factor is that, at first, you will probably have enough money to last you for awhile — not forever, but for awhile. Finally, some things in Thailand are not easy to get accomplished. I have already discoursed about going to the bank or post office or government office. These things would be time-consuming even if you were fluent in the Thai language. Since you probably aren't, they can turn into major projects that you'd rather not take care of today.

I have no solution for the habit of procrastinating beyond what common sense tells us all. People need to work and feel productive. It adds meaning and purpose to our lives. Work does not necessarily mean having a job. It means having projects and accomplishing things. A project is something that projects our being into the future. Earlier I related a story about a guy who was constantly *going* to do something but never did. He returned home disillusioned as well as broke. It is easy to be that kind of person, and the only thing that will prevent it is following through on your ideas — at least some of them. It is unrealistic to expect the enthusiasm that you started your adventure with to be your constant companion. You will have your ups and downs. By all means, however, avoid being an "all talk and no action" ex-pat.

Relative to the negative emotions described above, as well as other ones, there are two very concrete things you can do. Remember, frequently *saying* things makes them real and gives them power. Talking negatively breeds negativity. Talking and thinking positively creates a helpful environment and makes things doable.

Second, avoid negative people. There are plenty of such ex-pats in Thailand. They are not good for you, for Thailand or for themselves. Not only can you judge people by the company they keep, but attitudes tend to rub off. Hang out with hostile, complaining types and you may just catch what they have. Negativity is very contagious. Hang out with upbeat, happy people and the odds are good that you'll stay positive yourself.

Thai people are essentially optimistic and enthusiastic. If you catch anything in Thailand, try to make it those qualities.

Chapter Fourteen
The Thai Language

A language reflects a people's spirit. It reflects its values, culture, philosophy and thinking. The Thai language sings. It is poetic — indirect, and filled with analogy. It is a language brimming with fun and humor. Thai is at once an improbable and simple and difficult and respectful language.

To know a language is to know a people. I am just a beginner.

For those living in Thailand, or even for frequent visitors, it is important to learn the language. If we don't, we are rendered virtually helpless. We are restricted to dealing only with those who speak our own language. We can never really know Thailand.

I am not anywhere approaching being fluent in spoken Thai. I have difficulty hearing the five different tones. I can only read a handful of the 44 consonants and 24 vowels in written Thai. So this chapter is not a Thai lesson. I am far from being qualified to give one. Rather, like much of this book, it contains some suggestions for how to *approach* the Thai language.

At First

The most important thing in learning any language is not to be shy. You must put your ego aside. You are going to make mistakes. Don't worry about it. People are going to laugh and it may seem that they are laughing at you. They aren't. Some of the mistakes you make will be funny. Not long after arriving in Thailand, I went around to some shops trying to buy eggs. The response I got was either laughter or looks of disbelief. I hadn't been asking for eggs at all. I had been asking for shit! One day I asked several people if they knew where I could get a traditional Thai massage. Again, laughter was the response. I'd been asking where I could get a mustache. Many of the mistakes you will make are quite funny. Don't be paranoid. Join in the laughter. Most of all, don't give up.

You must, of course, buy a dictionary. There are scores of Thai/English dictionaries. I suggest that you get two. A bigger one to keep at home, and a smaller one to take with you. Make sure they are English/Thai as well as Thai/English. Try to find at least one that contains the following:

1. In the English/Thai section, it has the English word first, followed by the word transliterated into Thai, followed by the actual Thai word. (The latter is important so you can show it to people and point.)

2. In the Thai/English section, it has the Thai word first, followed by Thai transliterated into English, followed by the word in English. This way, your friends can point at the word, you can say it in Thai and understand what it means in English.

3. A few dictionaries even have an alphabetical section (in English) of transliterated Thai words so that, for example, if you hear someone say "rot fai" you can look it up in English and find out it means "train."

You will also want to buy a book on learning Thai — or, perhaps one that includes a cassette. There are scores of these, too Be careful in selecting one. Make sure it suits your needs and is a good one. There are a number on the market that aren't particularly helpful.

The best book for learning Thai that I have found is *The New What You See Is What You Say Thai Phrase Handbook* (see Important Reading, p. 137.). This is an excellent book in a sea of substandard also-rans. It has the very best transliterations I have seen anywhere, and is filled with useful phrases and pertinent illustrations, as well as a great deal of interesting cultural information.

You may want to take Thai language lessons at a school. I suggest that you learn a little of the language before you start, just so you have a foothold. Many private schools all over the country offer Thai language lessons. The cost ranges from $100 a month to $200 a month and up for a one-hour lesson, five days a week. Before you invest the money, make sure that you are truly committed to learning. The dropout rate is high. Also, make sure that the teacher is willing to teach you what you want to know, the way you want to learn it. Much of Thai education, including that at private language schools, involves rote learning and memorization. That is something you can probably do on your own, and it is not particularly helpful relative to learning conversational Thai. If you primarily want to learn to speak Thai, make sure the school understands that.

A Few Pointers

Obviously, when you are learning Thai, you'll want Thais to speak to you slowly. What you may not know is that it is best if *you* speak Thai slowly to them as well. Many times I have not been understood at first. When I slowed down, I was immediately understood.

Don't be self-conscious about walking around with a dictionary or phrase book. It is a great conversation starter.

Learn how to say some things that are not in the typical traveler or ex-pat vocabulary. It can be a lot of fun. In addition, try to learn more than merely bar Thai. If you spend any time in bars at all, you will pick up a lot of the jargon. Fine. But go beyond that.

Make it a point not to learn foul-mouthed (dirty) Thai. Not only can it get you in trouble, but as a non-native speaker you aren't really aware of the power and connotations of these words — even if you think you are merely using them in a joking manner.

Do not be a show-off or know-it-all when it comes to the Thai that you do know. I remember a guy in Pattaya who complained about how stupid Thais are because they couldn't understand him when *he spoke* Thai. Absurd, but true.

Don't hesitate to learn Thai from other farangs. Even if they don't know the language as well as you do, they may know a few things that you don't. A lot of the Thai I have learned came from other farangs. Don't let your ego get in the way here, either.

Teaching English to Thais can be a great way to learn Thai. There is no law against someone teaching for free or in exchange for Thai lessons.

Once you have learned some Thai, don't make a fool out of yourself showing it off. Showing off in Thailand is frowned on even more than in the West. As a general rule, I speak Thai with those whose English is worse than my Thai, and English with those whose English is better than my Thai. There are exceptions, of course. In less-touristed areas, you will occasionally meet someone who speaks only a little English and wants to practice. Do them a favor and speak English with them. Talk slowly and only make corrections if absolutely necessary or requested.

Because Thai is a tonal language and it is difficult for farangs to pick up those tones, be patient with yourself. Many times when I learned something new, it took a lot of practice before I was understood. Keep at it. Don't be offended if you're not understood or if you are corrected.

If you learn a little bit of the Thai alphabet, it will help you immensely in your pronunciation. There are charts and small books with the basic pronunciation, along with pictures to jog your memory.

Thai transliterated into English has no set rules of spelling or phonetics. You'll see things spelled many different ways. Obviously, a person who speaks American or Canadian English might spell something differently than an Englishman or Aussie. For example, Porn is a fairly common Thai nickname. As an American, I would be much more inclined to spell the name Pawn. Keep these spelling differences in mind when referring to a dictionary or reading English-language books about Thailand.

Most of the time, "h"s following a consonant are not pronounced, just as it isn't in the word "Thailand." Phuket is Poo-ket, not foo-ket.

There are some sounds in Thai that are very difficult for farangs to get. For example, the Thai alphabet has a letter that sounds like "dt" — about half way between a "d" and a "t" sound. By the same token, Thais have difficulty with some English sounds. For example, it is often hard for them to say sounds that involve two consonants together. The "th" sound is one. The soft drink Sprite is most often pronounced Sa-prite, and you may not be understood if you ask a waitress for a Sprite. In the Thai spoken by most people, words that are frequently transliterated with a "R" really sound more like an "L." For example, "I don't know" will be transliterated as "Phom mae rue." It usually sounds more like "Pome my loo." Even the word "farang," used a lot in this book, often sounds more like "falahng."

Thai does not have gender-specific impersonal pronouns. The word for he, she, him and her is "khao." It *does* have gender-specific *personal* pronouns. Be careful with the way you refer to yourself or you might just get a well-deserved chuckle. Also in this regard, Thai has two particles that are frequently added to sentences to make them more polite. A man would say "sawadee krap[1]" and a woman "sawadee ka," when saying, "Hello."

Thai has four different dialects: Central, Southern, Northern and Northeastern. Officially, Central (or Bangkok) Thai is the primary dialect.

As far as learning the Thai language goes, it can be summarized as follows: The grammar is easy. There are no verb conjugations, articles, prefixes, suffixes or gender (like Spanish, French or German has). Vocabulary and syntax are fairly easy. Pronunciation is difficult, but with practice you will be understood. Reading is quite hard, and writing even harder.

One final note. For some time now, I have been of the opinion that I spoke much better Thai after I had consumed a fair amount of alcohol. As if to corroborate this, I read in Michael Buckley's excellent *Bangkok Handbook*[2] that a study in the States showed that Americans did much better pronouncing Thai after they had drunk an ounce of alcohol. Perhaps it flies in the face of logic, but to me that means several ounces would be even better. Try it yourself.

---

1 This is transliterated most often as "krap" but is pronounced more like "kop."
2 Moon Publications, Chico, CA,1992.

Farangs can practice their Thai language skills with street vendors.

Chapter Fifteen
Sex

WARNING: This chapter may piss you off — especially if you are anything vaguely resembling politically correct. Of course, if you're politically correct, you may want to read what I have to say. Most P.C.ers seem to enjoy finding things to get pissed-off about.

This chapter is about *SEX!* I will tell you the what, when, where and how much of sex in Thailand. I make no judgments about the issue. I will leave it up to your imagination to determine what I have personally done — if anything. In my view, whatever people do sexually is strictly up to themselves. Some things are not to my taste and some things I don't like (like live sex shows in upstairs venues in Patpong, for example). But to each their own.

There is one major exception to the statement above. I *do* make a judgment about sex with children. It is absolutely and totally morally wrong. Period. Don't do it. More about that below.

Sex, like nearly everything else under the sun, is for sale in Thailand. Of course, it is for sale almost everywhere else on the globe, too. It's just that the Western media seem to enjoy making a big deal about sex in Thailand. That's because of three things.

First, Thais aren't as hypocritical as Westerners are about it. They know that most people have sex and enjoy sex, and that it is part of life. Second, the Western media, underscoring the hypocrisy, know that sex sells. They sell it in magazines, newspapers, TV and movies. That it's sold in the flesh in the West is glossed over, channeled into socially-acceptable but expensive mating rituals, covered up, criminalized, politicized and most of all lied about. Finally, there is the hysteria about AIDS. No one I know of denies that AIDS exists and that it is a major problem in most of the world. The media, however, again seem to have singled out Thailand. Yes, there is AIDS in Thailand. But it is not as big of a problem as the Western media would like you to believe. In Phuket, for example, it is far more dangerous to drive a motorbike than it is to have unprotected sex. Last year 350 people died in road accidents there — far more than the number of AIDS deaths. By all means practice safe sex. By no means believe that every other Thai has AIDS.

I hope that you can do two things prior to reading this chapter: First, forget everything you have ever encountered in the Western media relative to sex in Thailand — especially the garbage on tabloid-TV "news" shows. Nearly everything you read or see was put together by people who came here with agendas firmly implanted in their minds before they made their very brief visits. Their stories were already written. Second, unless you have been here or similarly honest places such as the Philippines, you have no comprehension of the sex industry in Thailand. There is *no* Western equivalent.

Sex Venues

There are a wide variety of ways to get sex in Thailand. Some you may have read about, others are a bit unusual. As a male in Thailand, you will run into sex everywhere you go, virtually from the moment you clear Customs at the airport. It is as unavoidable as the air we breathe.

Touts

Your first encounter with sex will probably be with a tout — a man claiming he can get a lady for you or take you to a good massage parlor. In Bangkok, where this happens most frequently, or Pattaya or Phuket where it occasionally happens, there is no reason to go through a tout. All it does is raise the price of things. Anything he is offering, you can easily find yourself for less money. Outside of these tourist destinations, the services of a middleman may be useful.

Nana Plaza by day (top). Sign in Nana Plaza says it all (bottom).

Go-Go Bars

There are three areas in Bangkok that have go-go venues catering to farangs. They are the infamous Patpong area, Nana Plaza on Sukhumvit Soi 4, and Soi Cowboy which runs between Sukhumvit Soi 21 and 23. Plainly stated, a go-go bar has dancing ladies.

The least desirable, most touristed, and most expensive area with the hardest and shrewdest women is Patpong. I rarely go to the go-goes there, and not many ex-pats do. If you decide to check Patpong out, I would suggest that you avoid upstairs bars touting shows. Most of them are rip-off joints. Most of the bars with King or Queen in the name are OK — King's Castle, for example.

Nana Plaza has gotten popular lately. It has some big-time Patpong-style go-goes, as well as some easygoing places. Nearly all of the bars have go-go dancers. Some places are fancy and have 30 or more girls dancing at one time — sometimes topless or even naked. Other places are smaller, and have only two or three girls dancing in bathing suits. I like the latter. The girls are usually friendlier and less demanding in the area of "lady drinks." Most high-powered go-goes in Bangkok charge more for their drinks. Beer, for example, is 70 baht (nearly $3).

Soi Cowboy, which used to run second to Patpong in terms of popularity, has dropped to number three. That's made it more appealing to me — fewer people, and consequently fewer girls with attitudes. Like Nana, there are big fancy places with lots of girls, and smaller, more laid-back places. Again, I prefer the latter.

Lady Drinks, Bar Fines And Sexual Service Prices

A good chunk of the money bar girls earn comes from lady drinks bought for them by customers. Most of the time these are soft drinks. Occasionally, a splash of Thai whiskey is added. Lady drinks average about 50 baht ($2), and the girl will get about 20 baht of that. It is consequently inevitable that you will be asked to buy a lady drink. Sometimes this happens quickly and aggressively, as at most of the places in Patpong. Sometimes a girl will sit with you for a long spell and never ask — as at some of the smaller places in Nana and Soi Cowboy. I *never* buy a drink for a woman who comes up to me and says, "Hello, how are you? What is your name? Where you stay? You buy drink for me?" Sometimes, after a few minutes of conversation, I will buy the girl a drink if she seems "nice." Usually, I wait longer than that. One ironclad self-imposed rule I have is that if I touch the girl — anywhere — I buy her a drink. If I don't touch her, I feel under no obligation whatsoever. I simply say, "No."

Don't think that you will walk into a go-go bar and immediately be swarmed over by women. Sometimes, one will come up quickly and, most often, this is the ugliest one in the joint. Usually, you will go in, sit down, order a drink and be left alone for awhile. If you see a girl you fancy, the secret to getting her over is eye contact and a smile. That will usually do the trick. Sometimes it doesn't. These girls are not interested in each and every man. They have standards and tastes, just as you do. They won't sit with just any ol' guy, and they certainly won't go with just any ol' guy.

If you find a girl you like and want to take her with you, a bar fine must be paid. The bigger and fancier the bar, the more the bar fine. In Bangkok, bar fines range from 250 to 375 baht ($10 to $15). In Phuket's beer bars, the bar fine is 100 baht ($4). The price you pay the girl herself should be negotiated before you pay the bar fine. Most Patpong girls won't go for less than 1,000 baht ($40) for a short time. Some girls at smaller places in Nana and Soi Cowboy will go all night for 500 baht ($20). Their prices will depend on how good-looking they are, how experienced they are, how much money they think you have, and how badly they need money. Remember, it is a business transaction. They are doing it for money. They may like you a little bit, but you are not particularly special to them.

You will notice that go-go girls wear a small tag with a number on it. That means that they work for the bar, that the bar has copies of their Thai I.D. card, and that they are of age. This is a protection for you. The odds of getting ripped off by a girl officially employed by a bar are minimal. But try to remember her number — mostly because you'll probably forget her name, and you may want to see her again.

Fancy hotels will either not let bar girls in at all or will charge you, officially or through a bribe, to get them in. Medium-priced hotels, which often cater to single men, may require the girl to leave her I.D. at the front desk, but there is no extra charge. Again, this is a protection for you. Your best protection is not to get so blind drunk that you lose your wits. If you tend to way overdo your boozing, take a buddy along with you to babysit. If you get pleasantly high or even kind of drunk, you will not have a problem. I have never had a problem with a Thai lady.

If you cannot take your companion back to your hotel or home, don't worry. There are plenty of inexpensive short-time hotels. Ask her. She'll know where to go.

Beer Bars

An odd name to be sure — sometimes made odder by reversing it to "bar beer." These are open-air bars which are usually a bit cheaper than go-goes. The girls don't dance, and wear ordinary, albeit sexy, clothing. They are more like hostesses. The atmosphere is more easygoing and the bar staff usually tries harder.

There is a group of beer bars across from Soi 1 on Sukhumvit. It runs parallel to the railroad tracks and is called "Buckskin Joe Village." There are some in Nana, as well as in Patpong. Most all of the bars in Phuket are beer bars. There are a few go-goes, but most aren't worth going to. Pattaya has a good percentage of beer bars, too.

The scenario with taking a girl from a beer bar is the same as go-goes: Bar fine and pay the girl — after services have been rendered, of course. Most places in Phuket don't do the "lady-drink thing." If the girl asks you for a drink, she is asking for an actual, factual drink. Most bars do, however, pay her a commission.

Generally speaking, the girls at beer bars are less aggressive and sometimes less experienced. Sometimes they are new to the trade. Sometimes they are older and have grown tired of the dancing and fast pace of go-goes. I suppose it's fair to say that your odds of finding a "nice girl" are slightly better at a beer bar. But again, do not get serious. It's strictly business.

Avoiding The Bar Fine: If it is near closing time (usually 2 A.M.) and you see no point in paying the bar because the girl has already done her job there, you may be able to save some money. Ask the girl if she'd like to go with you. If she does, tell her you don't want to pay the bar fine. Then, if she doesn't suggest it herself at this point, ask her if she'll meet you somewhere outside the bar. Frequently she will.

A Note About Pidgen English: It never ceases to amaze me that some guys think a girl who speaks limited English is going to understand a very complicated sentence with a heavy vocabulary. Don't expect to be understood if you say, "It's nearly two o'clock in the morning and I'd prefer to not pay the bar fine. Could we possibly meet somewhere?" Rather say, "I want go with you but I no want pay bar." Get to the point with a minimal number of (big) words.

Massage Parlors

All tourist areas and all cities of any size have massage parlors. In Bangkok, the signs are most often in English. In the provinces, they may only be in Thai. In that case, the way you find one is through a samlor driver or tuk-tuk. You simply say, using your new ability to speak pidgen, "I want lady massage."

Most massage parlors are fairly fancy. There is usually a sitting area for customers and a glassed-in area for the ladies. While you drink a beer, you can look at the numbered ladies behind the glass. You can take your time or pick one immediately. It is an interesting spectacle to watch, actually. I advise taking your time.

When you're ready, tell the man the number of your choice. The lady will come out and escort you to your room. You will be bathed, massaged, and have your sexual appetite gratified. After your bath, you can have conventional sex preceded by foreplay that includes the lady taking care of condom use in a very unobtrusive and erotic manner. If you are not satiated during conventional sex (in any position you may desire), the encounter will progress on to oral sex, which, in a massage parlor, is usually part of the treatment. Do not confuse a massage parlor with an establishment that clearly advertises "traditional Thai massage." At the latter, you may possibly get a hand-job, at best; at worst, you'll make a fool of yourself.

Your trip to the message parlor will cost you between 1,000 and 2,500 baht ($40 to $100). 99% of the time it will be highly professional.

My taste doesn't run toward massage parlors. I find it artificial (yeah, I know, so what isn't?), and it actually makes me kind of nervous and shy. There is no reason why you should feel that way, however. If it's a "rub and scrub" you want, go for it. If you're a bit nervous about it, that's understandable. These women have a knack for putting you at ease though.

Coffee Shops, Discos and Other After-Hours Places

Actually, there are several different kinds of Thai coffee shops, none of which are known for their coffee. Another kind is described below under the label "Sing-a-Song Places."

In Bangkok and others places with a substantial population of farangs, the bars close at 2 AM, but the action doesn't stop. Among the ways around the closing time is to have a restaurant or "constellation" (usually a disco). The former are "coffee shops" where some food is available, but most people go to continue drinking. Discos are also allowed to stay open a bit later. I'm going to concentrate on coffee shops because, as a disco duck, I stopped quacking years ago. My advice for both is essentially the same.

The best-known coffee shop in Bangkok is the Thermae, located at about Soi 15 on Sukhumvit Road. Note that it is one of the few establishments I've mentioned by name. That's largely because it has been there for at least 25 years. It's a fixture. Bars and other establishments tend to change hands often, and there is a big turnover in staff.

If you don't know what you're looking for, the Thermae may be hard to find after-hours. They operate semi-legally; in conjunction, of course, with the police.

First, look for the food stalls on the sidewalk. Then look to see if there is a sign on the building that says "Thermae Turkish Bath." Walk down the alley to the left of the building, and you'll enter through the toilet. Walk down several stairs, then down the hall, and enter a room the likes of which you have never seen in your life. This is the nadir of sleaze. Paunchy middle-aged men, usually drunk, eyeing Thai ladies who are usually considerably younger and better-looking than the guys doing the looking. The secret here is all in the eye contact and smile. Do that, and the ball is rolling. The women here are freelancers or go-go girls who didn't hook a guy at work, or, occasionally, girls who have proper daytime jobs and want some extra cash. There are, believe it or not, some pretty nice women at the Thermae. In any case, it is a must for connoisseurs of sleaze.

Sing-A-Song Places

You will find these venues all over Thailand. In addition to the gaudy lights outside, there are usually pictures of the women on the outside wall. The women are ostensibly singers. Some of them aren't bad either, and occasionally the places are actually respectable. The way things work here, in addition to the ever-present smiling and ogling, is to buy the singer some flowers (usually artificial, so they can be sold again and again), and present them to her while she is singing. After that, it's up to you.

Hotel Sex

If you check into a hotel in the provinces, you will probably be asked by the elevator operator or bellboy if you want a lady. If you do, say yes, but be specific about what you want. The price will run from $20 to $30, with the lady generally leaving about 7 or 8 in the morning. If it is an all-nighter you want, make sure that is clear ahead of time. Tuk-tuk drivers or bicycle samlors will also take you to brothels where the women are as cheap as $4. In the provinces, you have little choice but to seek assistance from a local.

The Thai Sex Scene

There are many places, both in Bangkok and elsewhere, that cater to Thai men. Westerners did not invent prostitution in Thailand. Simply because it is a Thai establishment does not mean that farangs aren't welcome. Most of the time these places are quite safe, although it is probably wise to go with a friend. Thai go-goes and karaokes are not much cheaper than places with a farang clientele. Thai brothels are much cheaper. There also happens to be something kind of sad about them.

The main Thai night-life area in Bangkok is on Sutisan Road. It is often referred to as the Thai Patpong. In my estimation, Sutisan is to be preferred over its farang equivalent.

The main drawback for many sojourners is that virtually none of the women in Thai establishments speak even rudimentary English. That makes things difficult. Until you learn enough to get by, it is probably best to take a friend along who knows the language.

Thai prostitutes are human beings. They have likes, dislikes and problems like anyone else. They should always be treated with kindness, dignity and understanding.

If you have a particular sexual activity that you enjoy that is beyond missionary style, you should check with the lady before you go with her. Many Thai women do not, for example, like oral sex. On the other hand, some specialize in it.

Condom use is important. If you don't like sex with a condom, remember that as long as you don't go *inside* a woman (in any of her orifices), neither of you can get a sexually-transmitted disease. Be creative. But be careful.

Alternative Sex

Gay sex, lesbian sex, threesomes and foursomes and bar girls going with a married couple are all possibilities. With anything "unusual" or out of the ordinary one-guy, one-girl stuff, you must always check ahead of time. Eye contact, jokes, buying drinks and then talking can get the ball rolling. If in doubt, check with the mamasun.

Sex and Children

The Western media have focused a lot of attention on the problem of sex with minors. That it is a problem is certainly true. But that Thailand has been singled out is grossly unfair. One of the most common questions I got asked the last time I was in the States was about child prostitutes. That is an image of Thailand which is wrong. If we think of child prostitution as child abuse, which it is in spades, Thailand has no more of a problem than any other country. But is it a problem? Yes.

In spite of serious crackdowns by the authorities, there are still minors working in the sex business. Many of these children are sold by their parents into a life of virtual slavery. Anyone who supports such exploitation — including people who patronize these places — is *scum*. Don't do it. In addition to that, there is a chance you'll be arrested. You wouldn't be the first. Furthermore, several countries have passed laws allowing prosecution back home for what is done in Thailand. In Sweden, for example, a 68-year-old man is in prison for sleeping with a 13-year-old boy prostitute in Thailand.

Summary: Some kind of sexual encounter in Thailand is virtually inevitable. That doesn't mean that you will actually have sex, but that something of a sexual nature will occur. Don't be a tightass about it. Enjoy it. Have fun with it. Marvel at it. If you feel like it, *do it*. But be careful, honest and frank but tactful. Make sure your expectations are grounded in reality — whether it comes from your heart or another organ. Don't go nuts with your money. Think before you screw. Move slowly. There are plenty of beautiful fish in the sea. There's always tomorrow — especially if you're an ex-pat living in Thailand.

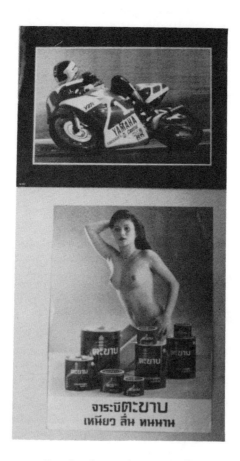

Speed and sex... that says it all.

Chapter Sixteen
Do's and Don'ts

Do

Smile a lot.

Say good things about Thailand, Buddhism and the Royal Family — they deserve it.

Be more patient than you've ever been in your life.

Learn to speak a little Thai — and not just "bar Thai." (Don't be a showoff about the Thai language that you do know, or get upset if you are not immediately understood.)

Learn how to say no — especially in a polite way.

Bargain for prices for everything, but with a happy and friendly attitude.

Get off the beaten track to the real Thailand occasionally.

Use condoms.

Accustom yourself to Thai toilets.

Bend down a little bit when walking in front of or between people.

Be as indirect as humanly possible if you must criticize.

Flatter people — especially if you must criticize something.

Learn to enjoy Thai food.

Participate in Buddhist ceremonies.

Wear decent clothing to temples, visits to Immigration or other offices, and in the evening.

Take your shoes off before going into temples or people's homes.

Wai (bow slightly with hands together in front of you) monks, old people and those with a higher standing than you.

Read the Trink Page in the Saturday *Bangkok Post*.

Do Not

Speak badly of, or make jokes about, Thailand, Buddhism or the royal family.

Wai children, bar girls or service workers. Do not even do it as a joke. These things are a sign of ignorance.

Mistake Bangkok, Patong Beach or Pattaya for Thailand.

Give people the finger or otherwise display anger in an aggressive way.

Pay bar girls more than 1,000 baht (500 is far better).

Tip cab or tuk-tuk drivers.

Give a bar girl your wallet to carry around and pay for things.

Buy drinks or give cigarettes to everyone who asks.

Make a problem with Thai men.

Count on any "deadline" being met.

Be afraid to ask for a better price on anything. Oftentimes, the real price for something (especially in a tourist destination) is one-fourth to one-half of the first price quoted. Paying too much hurts other ex-pats.

Loan money to anyone (including ex-pats).

Buy drugs — especially from someone you don't know (e.g., tuk-tuk driver). As this book was going to press, it was reported that an American man had been sentenced to life imprisonment for attempting to smuggle heroin out of Thailand.

Buy gold for bar girls.

Touch people on the head, even in a joking manner.

Expect your girlfriend not to return to the bar after you've gone home — even if you send her money (which you should not do either).

Do favors with the expectation that favors will be returned. You do kind things because you want to, and it is you who makes merit.

Whine and cry and expect sympathy.

Buy a bar or condo.

Expect your money to arrive from home into your Thai bank account quickly — even if it is a wire transfer.

Talk about how much better your home country is than Thailand.

Expect people to say "thank you" a lot.

Expect to be introduced to everyone who comes along.

Make a scene in public with your girlfriend, shopkeepers, etc.

Make a public show of affection — kissing, hand holding, etc.

Chapter Seventeen
Final Thoughts

Flexibility, spontaneity and acceptance.

Almost nothing in this book is set in concrete. Siam Cement.

Most everything I have said is flexible and no doubt debatable. There are a lot of gray areas. If, for example, I have emphasized watching your money too much, it is simply because in my own experience, I have seen foolish and wasteful farangs ruin their own lives and indirectly hurt other farangs. You should not be a tightwad either — a real Cheap Charlie. Generosity is important in life.

Some of the things I have said, especially in the do's and don'ts section, you will see done or not done (as the case may be) all the time. You'll see blatant displays of public affection, people wearing shorts in temples and other such things. Just because other people do it does not mean it is the polite or decent thing to do. Just because you're a farang and can get away with it, doesn't mean you should. But you have to decide things for yourself. If you want to wear flip-flops, a Hawaiian shirt, short pants and sandals around Bangkok at night, by all means do so.

Some things are not in the Hawaiian shirt category.

An acquaintance of mine was visiting us when we lived in Phuket. We were both sitting in chairs and my son, who was about one year old at the time, came tottering over. My "friend" took his foot and touched my son's head. My wife didn't say anything. I did.

"That's just about the worst thing you can do to a Thai."

"Yeah," he said, laughing, "that's why I did it."

I didn't find the humor in it, and neither did my wife. She was convinced that my son's fussiness for the next several days was a result of the head (high)/foot (low) -touching incident. She never had anything to do with the man again. He became invisible for her.

A fellow I know was working on a fairly big business deal involving importing a certain item from Germany. He went to see a high-ranking Customs official. The farang wore a tank top, short pants and flip-flops. His requests for licenses, etc. were turned down on the spot.

There is no substitute for using your head and taking the middle path. If you don't know what to do, ask a Thai. If there is no one to ask, do nothing. If you don't know what to say, say nothing and smile. If you must do or say something, that is the time to be grateful — very grateful — that Thai people are tolerant and understanding.

Comments in the book about not buying gold for bar girls or getting involved in a bar or loaning people money are not written in stone, either. They are meant to be guidelines, not laws or commandments. You must always use your own judgment. I have provided what I call guidelines because Thailand is such an extraordinary place that it is easy to lose your judgment and common sense. It is a place that truly does inspire awe. Sometimes when we are awed by something, it is difficult to think straight and be rational.

By the same token, simply because you should be careful with criticism or anger does not mean that those things are never, ever appropriate. Sometimes, even in Thailand, they are quite appropriate. The trick, of course, is to figure out when. That is true of a lot of things I have stated in this book. So, once you begin to know where you are, you can change some of the "nevers" in this book to "when the time is right."

There are a couple of things that *are* written in stone. These things involve the Royal Family or Buddhism.

Under no circumstances talk badly about the King and his family. Honestly, you should never have reason to anyway. They are exceptional people and should you speak badly about them, you are not only acting stupidly, but you are mistaken as well.

Buddha and the monks are the fabric that holds this fine country together. There is no reason to say or do anything bad in this area, either. If common decency and intelligence aren't enough to convince a person of the importance of these things, they should know that it is against the law to speak badly about the king or be disrespectful toward Buddha images. People, including farangs, go to jail for doing so. The time in jail could end up being several weeks or more, *if* you are able to buy your way out quickly. If not, it could easily extend into months.

The author and a Thai cave monk.

Being positive about all things Thai — about everything on your adventure — will translate into positive results. That is more true in Thailand than it is in the West. Thai people appreciate life and generally exude a happy and friendly attitude, even when they are beset by problems. I hope that rubs off on you.

Finally, it is my deep and sincere opinion that because this is Thailand, every single benefit of every doubt ought to go to the Thai way of thinking and doing things. I hope that you did not consider some of the discussions in this book negative. The sections about waiting at the bank, or lack of consumer protection, or money were in no way intended as criticisms. As I stated in the introduction, we are *guests* in this country. Not only should we try to do as Thais do, we should try to understand, adapt and learn. Learning is the reason for all adventures. It may even be the reason for life itself.

Glossary
of Ex-Pat Lingo

This is a list of words and phrases used in the book and frequently by ex-pats. For Thai words, your best bet is a phrase book. Lonely Planet publishes a good one.

Ajarn — Teacher. Sounds more like ajohn to an American.

Amarit — A Thai beer.

Baht — Thai money, approximately 25 baht to the dollar.

Baksheesh — A Persian word, used by Thai ex-pats to refer to a bribe or expected tip.

Bar fine — Money you pay a bar to "release" a bar girl or go-go dancer for the night.

Bar girl — Woman in the field of sexual services who works at a bar.

Buddha — Strictly speaking, Siddhartha Gautama, the founder of Buddhism. In practice, any revered figure in Thai history, and sometimes Hindu gods or goddesses. Occasionally, when talking to a farang, a Thai will call a monk "buddha" because they don't know the word for "monk," which, in Thai, is "phra."

Butterfly — Promiscuity and/or infidelity.

Chiang Mai — Northern Thailand's major city, which has long been a tourist destination, but is suffering growing pains, not the least of which are traffic jams and pollution.

Coffee shop — A place where ladies sing songs and offer other services or an after-hours place.

Double-pricing — Higher prices for farangs than Thais.

Ex-pat — Short for expatriate, a person living outside their "home country." "-Pat" rhymes with "fat."

Farang — A non-Asian foreigner.

Go-go dancer — Woman in the field of sexual services who does a lot of dancing in a bathing suit or various stages of undress.

Issan — Northeast Thailand, with a unique culture, food and language. Sometimes spelled Isaan, Esan or Isan.

Katoy — Transsexual (full-blown or in transition), or transvestite.

Kee-neow — Cheap Charley, tightwad.

Key money — Up-front lump sum payment for the "privilege" of leasing a property.

Kloster — A Thai beer.

Ko Samui — Thailand's third largest island. It is changing rapidly, but it is still more of a hippie destination than many other places.

Krung Tep — The way Thais refer to Bangkok.

Lady drink — A small drink you buy for a bar girl. Usually it has no alcohol, and she gets a commission.

Lao Kao — Issan whiskey made from rice. Watch out!

Mai pen rai — Never mind.

Mekong — Thai whiskey with — sometimes — unusual effects, including bizarre dreams.

Monkey house — Thai jail. No fun, no frills.

Motorbike taxi — Useful, especially in Bangkok, because of the traffic, but extremely dangerous. Activate nerves of steel before departure. Negotiate price first.

Muay thai — Thai kick-boxing.

Nana Plaza — Night life and go-go area on Sukhumvit Soi 4.

Pattaya — Sexual playground about two hours by bus from Bangkok.

Patong — Town on the island of Phuket in Southern Thailand known for its nice beach and raucous night life.

Patpong — Heavily touristed, expensive and aggressive nightlife and go-go area in Bangkok.

Penang — Malaysian island near Southern Thailand that is a popular place for turnarounds and visa runs.

Phee — Ghost.

Phra — Monk.

Phuket — Popular tourist destination in Southern Thailand. The island offers something for everyone.

Ring the bell — Ringing the bell in a bar means you buy a drink for everyone — even if you thought you were just joking.

Samlor — Three-wheel, rugged and slow, motorcycle taxi found in Northeast Thailand. There are also tricycle samlors. Negotiate price first.

Sangria — Community of monks.

Sangthip — Slightly-decent Thai whiskey.

Sawadee — Similar to "hello."

Sticky rice — Issan-style rice. Eaten with the fingers.

Shooter — Mini-"cocktail," usually combining several kinds of booze. Served in a fancy shot glass.

Short time — Quickie sex.

Short-time hotel — Place to go for a short time.

Singha — Thailand's most popular beer. Besides regular Singha, they brew a Singha Gold and Singha Draft which are preferred by many farangs.

Soi — A smaller street intersecting a larger one. Numbered consecutively with an odd-numbered side of the street and an even-numbered side.

Soi Cowboy — Go-go and night-life area between Sois 21 and 23 off Sukhumvit in Bangkok.

Taxi meter — Metered and very economical taxis initiated in Bangkok a couple of years ago. Make sure the driver turns the meter on.

Thermae — After-hours coffee shop, restaurant and pick-up joint located near Sukhumvit Rd. Soi 15 in Bangkok.

Tilac — Sweetheart. Pronounced "tee-lack."

Trink — Bernard Trink, author of the popular and useful "Trink Page" in the Saturday *Bangkok Post*.

Tuk-tuk — 3-wheel Bangkok taxi. Negotiate price before going.

Turn-around — An exit and re-entry into Thailand in order to activate another three months on your multiple-entry visa.

Visa — Magic stamp in your passport that allows you to stay in Thailand.

Visa run — A trip out of the country to get a new visa.

Wat — Buddhist temple.

Wai — Hands together (prayer-like). A sign of respect, greeting or thanks. The higher the wai, the more respect.

Work permit — Government permission to work in the country. Without it, you are subject to arrest.

Wat Arun, Bangkok.

Jmportant Reading

Allyn, Eric. *The New What You See Is What You Say Thai Phrase Handbook,* Bangkokj, Bua Luan Publishing Co., 1993. (Distributed in the US by Orchid House, 2215-R Market St., #829, San Francisco, CA 94144. (415) 749-1100.)

Asia Books Guides. Bangkok, Asia Books. Asia Books publishes a series of guide books. One is for Thailand itself. There are separate guides for Phuket, Bangkok and Chiang Mai. All are filled with essential information.

Buckley, Michael. *Bangkok Handbook,* Chico, CA, Moon Publications. This is a guide published by Moon Publications, the same people who did the Carl Parkes book mentioned below. Very well done.

Cooper, Robert and Nanthapa. *Culture Shock! Thailand,* Singapore: Times Books, 1982. This is part of a series of Culture Shock books. It is invaluable reading for anyone living in Thailand and should be re-read every couple of years. It is aimed more at executive types than adventurers.

Hollinger, C. *Mai Pen Rai,* Boston, Houghton Mifflin. This is a classic and enjoyable book.

Parkes, Carl. *Thailand Handbook,* Chico, CA, Moon Publications. There are numerous travel guides to Thailand. Carl Parkes's is one of the best because it is thorough and honest. In addition to being a travel guide, it has a lot of information on Buddhism, climate, temples, schooling and more.

Segaller, Dennis. *Thai Ways,* Bangkok Post Publishing. This book and its two sequels are collections of essays about Thai culture, religion, language, customs, politics and more. These three books are essential to have in your library. A treasure trove of information collected by a man who has lived in Thailand since 1965.

ADDITIONAL READING

Burtt, E.A., editor. *The Teachings of the Compassionate Buddha: Early Discourses, the Dhammapada, and Later Basic Writings,* New American Library, 1955. This book has been around a long time but is one of the best anthologies, in English, of Buddhist texts.

Conze, Edward, editor. *Buddhist Scriptures,* Viking Penguin, 1959.

Cummings, Joe. *Thailand: A Travel Survival Kit,* Lonely Planet Guides, 1992.

Harshananda, Swami. *Hindu Gods and Goddesses,* Mysore, India, Sun Publishing, 1982.

Herman, A.L. *A Brief Introduction to Hinduism: Religion, Philosophy & Ways of Liberation,* Westview, 1991. Understanding Hinduism will help you understand Buddhism.

Hinds, John. *Faces of the Night,* Bangkok, Thai Press, 1989. Realistic short stories about nightlife in the City of Angels.

Jumsai, M.L. Manich. *Understanding Thai Buddhism*, Bangkok, Chalermnit, 1971.

Mahathera, Nyanatiloka. *Karma and Rebirth*, Chiang Mai, Thailand, 1988.

Mascaro, Juan, translator. *Upanishads*, VikingPenguin Press, 1965.

Maugham, W. Somerset. *The Razor's Edge*, Viking Penguin, 1992. Maugham can be stodgy at times, but this is a classic story of one man's search for understanding. The original motion picture is better than the remake.

Northrop, F.S.C. *The Meeting of East and West: An Inquiry Concerning World Understanding*, Ox Bow, 1979. A classic study that influenced, among other people, Robert Pirsig.

O'Merry, Rory. *My Wife in Bangkok: AIDS and Prostitution in Thailand*, Asia Press, 1990. An interesting, albeit short, tale of one American's experience with living and loving in Bangkok.

Pirsig, Robert M. *Zen & the Art of Motorcycle Maintenance: An Inquiry Into Values*, William Morrow, 1979. I don't need to say anything about this modern classic except read it if you haven't.

Radhakrishnan, Sarvepalli. *The Hindu Way of Life*, Harper, San Francisco, CA, 1988.

Reps, Paul and Senzaki, Nyogen, editors. *Zen Flesh, Zen Bones: A Collection of Zen & Pre-Zen Writings*, Shambhala Publications, 1994. Probably the best small and affordable collection of Zen writings.

Schumacher, E.F. *Small Is Beautiful: Economics As If People Mattered*, HarperCollins, NY, 1989. Still relevant and readable. Helpful insights into "peasant" economics.

Smith, Huston. *The World's Religions: Completely Revised and Updated Edition of The Religions of Man*, Harper, San Francisco, 1991. I don't agree with all that Smith has to say, but this is a nice basic book on comparative religion.

Wurlitzer, Rudolph, *Hard Travel To Sacred Places*, Shambhala Publishing, 1994. A beautifully woven tale of two lovers' anguished search for Buddhist enlightenment and tranquility in modern Indochina.

YOU WILL ALSO WANT TO READ:

"Loompanics is visionary..."
— **Village Voice**

"Books that test the First Amendment the way a bad child tests a permissive parent."
— **The Orlando Sentinel**

"Fully indexed, graphically laid out, the Loompanics catalog is a real shopping trip. And well worth it... a natural for small press people."
— **Small Press Review**

"An astonishing line of books..."
— **The Washington Post**

"Here are books that are very definitely *not* at your local library or bookstore."
— **The Whole Earth Catalog**

"Loompanics is probably the most radical catalog and press of all...."
— **City Paper**

"Scary..."
— **Publisher's Weekly**

"Serving millions of fringe info-gatherers daily... Loompanics Unlimited is the Looney Tunes of totally cool texts... the hepcats of out-there-lit."
— **Spin**

THE BEST BOOK CATALOG IN THE WORLD!!!

We offer hard-to-find books on the world's most unusual subjects. Here are a few of the topics covered IN DEPTH in our exciting new catalog:

- *Hiding/Concealment of physical objects! A complete section of the best books ever written on hiding things.*
- *Fake ID/Alternate Identities! The most comprehensive selection of books on this little-known subject ever offered for sale! You have to see it to believe it!*
- *Investigative/Undercover methods and techniques! Professional secrets known only to a few, now revealed to you to use! Actual police manuals on shadowing and surveillance!*
- *And much, much more, including Locks and Lockpicking, Self-Defense, Intelligence Increase, Life Extension, Money-Making Opportunities, Human Oddities, Exotic Weapons, Sex, Drugs, Anarchism, and more!*

Our book catalog is 8½ x 11, packed with over 500 of the most controversial and unusual books ever printed! You can order every book listed! Periodic supplements keep you posted on the LATEST titles available!!! Our catalog is $5.00, including shipping and handling.

Our book catalog is truly THE BEST BOOK CATALOG IN THE WORLD! Order yours today. You will be very pleased, we know.

LOOMPANICS UNLIMITED
PO BOX 1197
PORT TOWNSEND, WA 98368

Name_____

Address_____

City/State/Zip_____

Now accepting Visa and MasterCard.
For credit card orders *only*, call 1-800-380-2230.
9am to 4pm, PST, Monday through Friday.